FEMINIST PHILOSOPHIES A–Z

Volumes available in the Philosophy A–Z Series

Christian Philosophy A–Z, Daniel J. Hill and Randal D. Rauser
Epistemology A–Z, Martijn Blaauw and Duncan Pritchard
Ethics A–Z, Jonathan A. Jacobs
Indian Philosophy A–Z, Christopher Bartley
Jewish Philosophy A–Z, Aaron W. Hughes
Philosophy of Language A–Z, Alessandra Tanesini
Philosophy of Mind A–Z, Marina Rakova
Philosophy of Religion A–Z, Patrick Quinn
Philosophy of Science A–Z, Stathis Psillos

Forthcoming volumes

Aesthetics A–Z, Fran Guter
Chinese Philosophy A–Z, Bo Mou
Islamic Philosophy A–Z, Peter Groff
Political Philosophy A–Z, Jon Pike

Feminist Philosophies A–Z

Nancy Arden McHugh

Edinburgh University Press

© Nancy Arden McHugh, 2007

Edinburgh University Press Ltd
22 George Square, Edinburgh

Typeset in 10.5/13 Sabon
by TechBooks India, and printed and
bound in Great Britain by
Antony Rowe Ltd, Chippenham, Wilts

A CIP record for this book is
available from the British Library

ISBN 978 0 7486 2217 7 (hardback)
ISBN 978 0 7486 2153 8 (paperback)

The right of Nancy Arden McHugh
to be identified as author of this work
has been asserted in accordance with
the Copyright, Designs and Patents Act 1988.

Contents

Series Editor's Preface

Philosophy has traditionally been a very male form of activity, surprising perhaps given its place as a humanities discipline. Most professional philosophers today are men, and while it is not difficult to produce a list of important thinkers from the history of philosophy, it is difficult for many philosophy students to think of any women to include in such a list. There were in the past many female philosophers, but they have on the whole not been treated as of equal value as their male peers. This volume does not look at these female thinkers, however, since feminist philosophy is not the activity of philosophy as carried out by women. It is rather philosophy developed in a way that makes the issue of gender and everything that stems from it an important and even crucial theoretical concept. For example, philosophy has traditionally set out to ignore the gender and race context within which thought was produced, working with a notion of objectivity and validity that transcends, or seeks to transcend, personal issues. The whole point of philosophy is to consider the arguments themselves and only peripherally the nature of the arguers, their cultural and social backgrounds, or so it was often argued. Feminist philosophy sets out to study philosophy within a particular context, the context in which it was produced and who produced it, and considers these issues of context as significant in assessing the nature of the activity itself. Many women in philosophy have contributed to this activity, and Nancy McHugh provides here an introduction to some of the basic language and personalities in the area. Some of this language has become technical and requires explication, since it is used to bring out aspects of argument and theory that traditional philosophy has for a long time ignored. Much of this language involves a new way of looking at philosophy and it is the intention of this guide to make this easier to grasp and operate.

Oliver Leaman

Introduction

Feminist Philosophies A–Z is a reference covering contemporary feminist philosophy. It is oriented toward students in feminist philosophy and women's studies classes as well as a general audience interested in feminist theory. The goal of the *A–Z Series* is to provide pithy coverage of important terminology and figures in philosophy. Because of this there is a fair amount of breadth in the volumes, with depth in some areas, but not all.

In *Feminist Philosophies A–Z* my goal is to have a representative coverage of the field as well as to focus on some areas of feminist philosophy. In this volume I have tried to be particularly conscious of areas of feminist philosophy that may have received less coverage in other references or are newer to feminist philosophy and are receiving increased coverage in feminist philosophy courses. For example, there are several entries devoted to debates in transnational feminism, Third World feminism and antiglobalisation. Furthermore, I have tried to show how debates in areas such as Chicana/Latina feminism, Black feminist thought and Third World feminism have informed other areas of feminist philosophy. Thus many general entries make reference to these areas to show the cross-fertilisation of ideas and make clear that feminist philosophy is an ongoing, critical practice that seeks growth and revision. The volume is also attentive to many of the ongoing debates and ideas in feminist philosophy. For example, there are entries on reproductive rights, reproductive technologies, postmodern feminism, radical feminism, Marxist feminism, the public/private distinction, feminist epistemology and feminist ethics.

For the most part, I cover figures that consider themselves self-consciously feminist. So all the entries reflect twentieth- and twenty-first-century feminism, even though there may be figures in the history of philosophy, such as Mary Wollstonecraft, that we now tend to talk about as feminist or having feminist ideals. I also include only women in this volume. Though there may be feminist men, for a variety of reasons I thought it was important to devote my limited space to the coverage of important women in feminist philosophy. I am sure that there are important female figures that I have left out. For this I apologise. There are so many women who have made significant and unique contributions to feminist philosophy, it is hard to give all of these figures the attention they are due. Because feminist philosophy still holds a marginal position in philosophy, all feminist work is noteworthy, is a challenge to the discipline and deserves recognition.

In regards to the entries, for each entry on a feminist philosopher or feminist thinker I include country of origin and race or ethnicity. I realise that this might make some readers uncomfortable, but I do it for a variety of interrelated reasons. Most feminists of colour identify their race or ethnicity because they view it as important to their theorising. Because their race or ethnicity is so central to their view of their work, I certainly wanted to include it in the description of their work. In doing so, it seems wrong not to include whiteness as a racial category for white feminist thinkers. Whiteness is a location from which white feminists theorise whether or not they are self-conscious of it. I didn't want to further other women of colour by identifying their race as part of their epistemological location and not recognise that whiteness is a privilege, a place from which white women theorise from and a place to critically interrogate. Quite frankly, it was not always an easy task to identify women as white, because, unlike most women of colour, most white feminists don't specifically identify racially or ethnically. I thus had to make some inferences that may be false. I recognise that this is problematic, but I think that the importance of not further othering women of colour and recognising the political and epistemological significance of whiteness outweighs these concerns.

In terms of use of this text, the references are organised alphabetically, not categorically. Most entries have terms within them that are in bold type. For example, in the entry on **anticapitalist critique** the reader will find in bold **Chandra Talpade Mohanty, anti-racist feminism, Marxist feminism, socialist feminism, globalisation** and **decolonisation**. The setting of terms in bold indicates that they are also included in this volume. Thus you can use the entries to cross-reference other entries in the volume. For some entries there are terms at the bottom that can also be cross-referenced. For example, the entry **anti-racist feminism** has at the end of it the following terms in bold: **anti-capitalist critique; race; racism; Third World feminism; transnational feminism**. Furthermore, within entries there are references to texts either by the feminist being covered or feminists who have written on the term being covered. For many entries there are citations for further reading at the end of the entry. This usually occurs when there is not a citation within the text of the entry. At the end of the book there is an extensive bibliography that gives full references for all citations. In addition, the references are primarily to books by feminist philosophers rather than articles, though there are some articles cited. I do this because books tend to be more accessible to students and those newer to philosophy.

As in the case of my inclusion of feminist philosophers and thinkers, I have tried to be as inclusive as possible in terminology, but I am sure that I have left some terms out that others will find important or gave less attention to a term to which another writer would have given more. Disagreements about terminology and significance are to be expected with a text that seeks to provide coverage of a field. I have attempted to be balanced and attentive to the pluralism of feminist philosophy. Most entries give examples of specific feminist responses to the topic or term. This does not imply that this example represents some consensus among feminists on this topic. Instead it indicates how a feminist has theorised about or used a term. The goal is to point readers to specific resources on a topic that they can pursue further on their own and to help students understand how feminists work through and theorise about their subject matter. Finally, many entries include quotes from particular feminist philosophers who work in that area. I do this so that readers are able to get a sense of the voice of specific feminists as they engage with their subject. I believe this will help students delve more deeply into the material and learn the process of reading philosophy, which is a challenge for many.

It is my hope that readers will find this volume useful and use it as an impetus to further explore feminist philosophy.

Acknowledgements

Thank you to Oliver Leaman, the series editor, for approaching me to write this reference text. A further thanks goes to him and Carol Macdonald at the University of Edinburgh Press for their patience while I completed this volume. Thank you to Ann Cothran for her help with the Simone de Beauvoir reference. The strength of her knowledge and the thoroughness of her help made me realise that retirement is incredibly intellectually stimulating and that you never get tired of a subject that you love. Alison Tyner Davis deserves much recognition. She worked as my research assistant and always seemed excited and interested in the project. I look forward to her future contributions to feminist theory. Tammy and Molly always deserve recognition for their beer, morning runs and willingness to listen to me. Finally, Arden and Patrick, for the wonderful presence of you in my life, I will always give thanks.

Nancy Arden McHugh

Feminist Philosophies A–Z

A

Abject: the abject is a term first used by French feminist **Julia Kristeva** in her 1980 book *The Powers of Horror*. Kristeva uses the term to indicate the visceral horror humans experience when confronted by those aspects of themselves and life that force them to acknowledge their own materiality. The abject is the experience of the fear and revulsion of one's own impurity and materiality. All bodily functions are abject, especially those associated with waste or decay. The corpse and the maternal body are used by Kristeva as primary examples of the abject. One's confrontation with a corpse, especially of a person to whom one is close, forces one not just to confront one's own death symbolically, but to experience and confront the horror of the possibility of one's death. The maternal body represents expulsion, fruitfulness and generative power that are repulsive and threatening to the **phallocentric** order. Abject is an especially useful concept for feminists because Kristeva argues that all female bodies are viewed as inherently abject by patriarchal culture. **Judith Butler** utilises the concept of the abject in *Gender Trouble* (1990) to talk about all bodies that are transgressive.

See **semiotic; symbolic**

Addelson, Kathryn Pyne: white US feminist philosopher specialising in ethics and philosophy of the social sciences. Addelson's interdisciplinary approach combines her interest in practical social issues and interactionist sociology. Interactionist sociology is a branch of sociology committed to understanding social processes contextually and interpretatively such that social processes form the context in which events and conflicts take place, while at the same time serving as a site of meaning and interpretation of activity. Addelson affirms this interdisciplinary approach in her two books *Impure Thoughts: Essays on Philosophy, Feminism, Ethics* (1992) and *Moral Passages: Toward a Collectivist Moral Theory* (1994). In *Moral Passages* Addelson argues for an understanding of ethics and knowledge as generated by communities/collectivities and argues against the individualist, authoritarian approach prominent in mainstream ethical theory. She applies this understanding to various social issues such as reproductive rights, including birth control, abortion and teen pregnancy, gay and lesbian rights, and classism.

Agency: to be viewed as an agent or have agency is to be viewed as having **reason**, rights and responsibility. One might refer to a person as a moral agent. What most thinkers mean by this is that a person is able to make reasonable moral decisions and that person is therefore responsible for her own actions. One could also talk about a person being an epistemological agent. To do so would mean that the person exercises reasonable thinking. Feminists have critiqued agency on several counts. Among them are feminists who have provided historical critiques of the view that women are incapable of **rationality** and therefore cannot be moral or epistemological agents. Because **patriarchal** views of women have perceived them not to be agents in these senses, these patriarchal views have held that women should not be afforded the same rights and responsibilities as men who are considered moral agents. **Nancy Tuana**'s *The Less Noble Sex* (1993), **Carole Pateman**'s *The Disorder of Women* (1990) and *The Sexual Contract* (1988) and **Luce Irigaray**'s *This Sex Which is Not One* (1985a) are among the numerous feminist texts that provide critiques of the view that women lack moral and/or epistemological agency.

Irigaray's text analyses the psychoanalytic view that women are incapable of making authoritative statements about their own sexuality. She says 'that the *feminine occurs only within models and laws devised by male subjects*' (1985a: 86) and that 'often prematurely emitted, makes him miss ... what her own pleasure might be all about' (1985a: 91). So it is as male subjects that psychoanalysts construct the feminine, but because the feminine is constructed under a male model that views women as incapable of understanding themselves, the model misrepresents what feminine sexual pleasure is. Irigaray argues that if the 'female imaginary were to deploy itself, if it could bring itself into play otherwise than scraps, uncollected debris,' it would represent itself in a plurality that represents the pluralism of female genitalia (1985a: 30). Thus women gain agency by speaking in this plural voice.

Pateman's *The Disorder of Women* traces the historical view that women were incapable of agency and thus not accorded political rights or political voice because as women they were viewed by **androcentric**, patriarchal society as inherently disordered, thus lacking the **objectivity**, **rationality** and neutrality **embodied** in masculinity. In *The Less Noble Sex* Tuana traces the argument against women's rationality, and thus against women having agency, from biblical creation stories through modern science, philosophy and medicine, arguing that narratives are continually reconstructed such that women always come out as lacking in all senses in comparison to the androcentric model of man as ideal. Tuana shows how western thought has constructed women's lack of agency in everything from reproduction – women are mere vessels or fertile grounds – through to their ability to participate in philosophical thought.

Alcoff, Linda Martín: Latina feminist philosopher specialising in feminist epistemology, race and gender identity, and Latina/o identity. Alcoff is the author of *Visible Identities: Race, Gender, and the Self* (2006) and *Real Knowing: A New Version of Coherence Theory* (1996), and the editor of *Identities: A Reader* (2002) and *Feminist Epistemologies* (1991). In *Visible Identities: Race, Gender, and the Self* Alcoff employs hermeneutics and phenomenology to make visible and salient the **embodied**, experiential nature of **race** and **gender** identities. Alcoff argues that identities can be oppressive, but they don't necessarily have to be so. Furthermore, to deny the existence of racial and gender identities 'divert[s] attention away from discriminatory practices and identity-based patterns of segregation and exclusion' (290).
    See **embodiment; oppression**

Analytic Feminism: a type of feminism that grew out of analytic philosophy. Analytic feminists use the methodology of analytic philosophy to approach feminist concerns. For example, most analytic feminists hold on to the idea of truth, rationality and justice as **universal** properties to think about feminist arguments concerning knowledge and rights. Among noted analytic feminists are **Helen Longino** and **Lynn Hankinson Nelson**.

Androcentrism: for something, such as a theory or a right, to be androcentric means that it centres on men or that it is biased because of its focus on men. For example, feminists have argued that the man the hunter theory of human evolution is androcentric because it not only is a narrative that centres around men, but it also ignores and denies important evidence about what women were doing in the same historical period. It thus tells a biased, androcentric story about what human life was like based on androcentric assumptions.

See **gynocentric; masculinist; phallocentric**

Anti-capitalist critique: **Chandra Talpade Mohanty** describes anticapitalist critique as the view that feminism and capitalism are incompatible if feminism has as a goal cultural, economic and political transformation. It is linked to **Marxist feminism** and **socialist feminism**, but is significantly more invested in **anti-racist feminist** strategies. It 'fundamentally entails a critique of the operation, discourse, and values of capitalism and of their naturalization through neoliberal ideology and corporate culture' (2003: 9). Anticapitalist critique is deeply critical of the corporatisation of daily life across the globe. It is intimately tied up with the project of **decolonisation** and is intrinsic to arguments against **globalisation**.

Anti-racist feminism: Anti-racist feminism is a term used by a number of feminists to describe the intersection between race and gender. Third World feminist **Chandra Talpade Mohanty** points to the importance of racialising feminism. Mohanty states that antiracist feminism 'is simply a feminist perspective that encodes race and opposition to racism as central to its definition' (2003: 253). She uses the term to counter the backlash against feminism while making feminism relevant in a charged global environment. Furthermore, anti-racist feminism makes clear the connections between how racial hatred leads to increased violence against and **oppression** of women. In a similar vein Zillah Eisenstein in *Manmade Breast Cancers* (2001) argues that 'antiracist feminist theory is the struggle to newly see, again and again, the emerging forms of sex/gendered racialization' (152). Anti-racist feminism is deeply connected to **anti-capitalist critiques**, arguments against **monocultures** and **transnational feminism.**

See **race; racism; Third World feminism**

Anzaldúa, Gloria (1942–2004): Gloria Anzaldúa was a Chicana lesbian feminist writer. She co-edited the ground-breaking anthology *This Bridge Called My Back: Writings By Radical Women of Color* (1981), which brought to the forefront of feminist theory the writings of Third World women. Her concern, and the concern of other contributors to this volume, was the silencing of **Women of Colour** by mainstream feminism. Her book *Borderlands/La Frontera* (1999), which combines writing in Spanish and English, prose and poetry, provides a critical analysis of the oppressive nature of US politics and colonialism and argues for the importance of knowledge generated from the 'borderlands,' a critical, epistemological location. Anzaldúa forges what she calls the new *mestiza* consciousness, which, through straddling two cultures, works to break down dualisms and boundaries. She also edited *Making Face, Making Soul/Haciendo Caras: Creative and Critical Perspectives by Feminists of Color* (1990) and *This Bridge We Call Home: Radical Visions for Transformation* (2002). Critical interviews with Gloria Anzaldúa are collected in *Interviews/Entrevistas* (2000) and critical writings about her work are anthologised in *EntreMundos/AmongWorlds: New Perspectives on Gloria Anzaldúa* (Keating, 2005).

See **Chicana feminism and Latina feminism; Third World feminism**

Atherton, Margaret: white US feminist specialising in history of philosophy. Atherton is the editor of *Women Philosophers in the Early Modern Period* (1994). Atherton has worked to bring female philosophers that have been lost from the **canon** of Modern philosophy back to the mainstream of Modern thought, showing how women such as Mary Astell, Damaris Cudworth Masham and Anne Conway were intellectually active in early Modern philosophy.

B

Background assumptions: Background assumptions are unrecognised assumptions that inform one's view of something. For example, a background assumption that many people of European decent hold is that Europe is the cradle of all legitimate culture. This assumption, **Eurocentrism,** infects many of the actions of its holders. Background assumptions are difficult to recognise and acknowledge because they are held so deeply by individuals and cultures that even when they are pointed out they appear to be normal and true.

Further reading: Longino (1990)

Barrett, Michèle: white British socialist feminist in sociology. Barrett is the author of *The Politics of Truth: From Marx to Foucault* (1991) in which she reframes for feminist theory Marx's notion of ideology of as 'economics of truth'. In light of increased attention to feminist issues that cannot be explained in terms of **class** oppression, Foucaultian understanding of a 'politics of truth' is able to explain a more complex matrix of **oppression** that affects women that are multiply situated. Barrett is also the author of *Women's Oppression Today: The*

Marxist/Feminist Encounter (1989) and *Imagination in Theory: Culture, Writing, Words, and Things* (1999). In the now classic and widely referenced text, *The Anti-Social Family* (1991), Barrett and Mary McIntosh articulate how the social ideal of the family masks the reality of family life and enables violence and abuse in the home.

See **Marxist feminism; socialist feminism**

Bartky, Sandra Lee: white US, feminist philosopher specialising in existential phenomenology. Bartky's 1991 *Femininity and Domination: Studies in the Phenomenology of Oppression* is one of the first books in feminist philosophy to provide a systematic, critical analysis of beauty and the **embodiment** of beauty ideals. Through an existential phenomenological account Bartky argues that the fashion-beauty complex alienates women from themselves by first replicating western hegemony's view of women as purely bodily and then through alienating women from 'control [over] the shape and nature these bodies take' (41). Women become obedient to the demands of fashion and culture and are docile in the face of these imperatives. In her more recent work *Sympathy and Solidarity: and Other Essays* (2002) Bartky again employs existential phenomenology to analyse beauty, as well as **whiteness**, ageing and racial guilt. Bartky is one of the founders of the **Society for Women in Philosophy**.

Beauvoir, Simone de (1908–86): Simone de Beauvoir was a French existentialist philosopher and the author of the important feminist text *The Second Sex* (1952). In *The Second Sex* Beauvoir sets out to address 'Why woman is the Other' (33). She argues that in all situations, perspectives and experiences woman is **Othered**. She thus argues against the biological, Freudian and Marxist monolithic responses to this problem that treat woman's status as

Other as the result of having a certain kind of body, a certain relation to her own body, or performing particular types of labour such as child care and cooking. Through an existentialist approach Beauvoir puts forth that 'One is not born, but rather becomes, a woman' (267). Man identifies himself as the norm because woman poses a threat to male selfhood, thus woman is constructed as Other and deviant, not self, and exists only in relation to man. Man sees woman's nature as essential, not constructed. Because women's otherness is not a result of women's essential nature, in a final chapter of *The Second Sex*, 'Liberation: The Independent Woman', Beauvoir argues that women's 'future remains largely open' and she is not powerless in her situation (714). She can refuse her status as 'Other' by becoming economically independent, creative, intellectual, sexually empowered, work toward social change, and not allow herself to experience herself as Other. In addition to Beauvoir's important contribution to feminist theory, Beauvoir adds significantly to the existentialist concept of the Other by developing this concept to explain social relations instead of only the individual relations Sartre seeks to understand (Simons, 2000). This formulation has been important in **postmodern feminism**. Some of Beauvoir's other works are *The Ethics of Ambiguity* (1967), which pursues the ethical implications of existentialism, and *America Day By Day* (1999), which is a study of **race** relations in the United States.

See **essentialism; social construction**

Further reading: Moi (1994); Simons (2006, 2000)

Benhabib, Seyla: Turkish-American feminist philosopher specialising in social and political philosophy from a Continental perspective. Benhabib's work in feminist social and political philosophy provides a critical analysis of current issues through figures in the history of philosophy, such as Immanuel Kant, G. W. F. Hegel and Hannah Arendt, and through her own incisive arguments. In her book *Situating the Self* (1992), Benhabib reformulates communitarian moral theory, developing a postmetaphysical, interactive **universalism** that situates reason in embodied, embedded, gendered selves that are members of discursive communities. Her recent work, *The Rights of Others* (2004), argues for a cosmopolitan approach – an approach that recognises global membership and the right of all humans to inalienable human rights – to global justice and the migration of peoples across borders. From this perspective and employing Hannah Arendt and Immanuel Kant, while critiquing John Rawls, Benhabib analyses world hunger, globalisation, the European Union and several late twentieth, early twenty-first-century political events. Benhabib is also the author of *Democracy and Difference* (1996a), *The Reluctant Modernism of Hannah Arendt* (1996b) and *The Claims of Culture* (2002).

Biological Determinism: biological determinism is the view that certain biological features determine either the totality of one's being (personality, appearance, likes and dislikes) or certain significant features of a person. Feminists have been particularly concerned about deterministic views of **gender, sexuality** and **race**. A biological determinist would argue that one's gendered behaviour is determined solely by genetics and that society has nothing to do with how and whether one exhibits certain gendered behaviour. For example, a biological determinist would argue that aggression in males is a natural, biological gendered trait. A person critiquing this view may argue that male aggression is the product of a society that promotes and values aggression in males.

Further reading: Fausto-Sterling (2000)

Biopower: French philosopher Michel Foucault used the term biopower to denote the exercise of control over bodies through regulatory systems and practices. In the *History of Sexuality* (1990) Foucault argues that the rise of capitalism and modern government necessitated a greater regulation of bodies that wasn't needed under sovereign rule because sovereign power needed only to threaten death to control its population. The state employs a series of regulatory controls over the population in the guise of protecting life. In doing so the state effectively guarantees its ability to inhibit certain kinds of life choices and in certain cases ends lives. Examples of biopower are those practices that seek to regulate family, health, **sexuality**, birth, death, security or movement. For example, Foucault points to census taking and **heteronormative** training as examples of biopower.

Further reading: Foucault (1990); McWhorter (1999)

Black Feminist Thought: Patricia Hill Collins in her 1991 book *Black Feminist Thought* defines Black feminist thought. Black feminist thought is a type of **standpoint epistemology** that originates from the insights of Black feminist intellectuals such as **Audre Lorde, Barbara Smith** and **bell hooks,** and the experiences of **oppression** and domination that are the legacy of slavery. It emphasises the importance of seeing Black women as **agents** of knowledge and recognising the partiality of all knowledge. Collins is careful to articulate the importance of linking together activism and oppression as well as the importance of social transformation in the development of Black feminist thought.

Further reading: Collins (2005, 2006); hooks (1981, 1984, 1994, 2000); Lorde (1980, 1983, 1984, 1995); Smith (2000a&b)

Bordo, Susan: white US feminist philosopher, specialising in aesthetics and philosophy of the body. Susan Bordo endeavours to make philosophy accessible to the wider public by not only writing on topics that are of interest to a popular audience, but by writing in a style that is accessible to the public. Bordo brought the body and eating disorders to the forefront of philosophical attention and made them a legitimate area of study with her book *Unbearable Weight* (1993), which was nominated for a Pulitzer Prize. In this text Bordo uses the lens of the gendered body to understand how advertising, media and cultural norms have taught women how to see their bodies. She states that 'culture – working not only through ideology and images, but through the organisation of the family, the construction of personality, the training of perceptions – as not singularly contributory but *productive* of eating disorders' (50). In her 2000 book, *The Male Body*, she analyses masculinity and male bodies from a feminist perspective, thus contributing to the growing field of masculinity studies. Her other books include *The Flight to Objectivity* (1987) and *Twilight Zones: The Hidden Life of Cultural Images from Plato to O.J.* (1999).

See **embodiment**

Braidotti, Rosi: white Italian feminist philosopher teaching in the Netherlands, specialising in embodiment, poststructualism and psychoanalysis. In *Metamorphoses: Toward a Materialist Theory of Becoming* (2002) Braidotti states that all of her books are connected by a question: 'how can one free difference from the negative charge which it seems to have been built into it?' (4). In her book *Nomadic Subjects* (1994) Braidotti provides a series of essays that consider the nomadic nature of subjectivity, in other words the multiple, situated, embodied 'critical consciousness that resists settling into social coded modes of thought and behavior' (5). This critical positioning allows Braidotti to assess everything from technology to the status of women's studies. She argues that nomadic subjectivity and the recognition of difference leaves feminists with a 'crucial political question ... how is this awareness – the recognition of differences – likely to affect the often fragile allegiance of women of different classes, races, ages, and sexual preferences?' (257). Furthermore, she asks how will this affect coalition building, consensus making and assessments of common interests and pertinent differences. Braidotti turns her recognition of multiplicity to feminist theories, arguing that with the rapid growth of feminist theories feminists need to establish a feminist genealogy to counterbalance the continual misogyny in academia. Braidotti is also the author of *Patterns of Dissonance* (1991).

See **embodiment; postmodern feminism**

Butler, Judith: white US feminist philosopher specialising in queer theory and postmodernism. Judith Butler is credited with initiating philosophical interest in **queer theory** with her book *Gender Trouble* (1990) as well as generating increased attention to postmodernism as both theory and methodology in Anglo-American philosophy. Butler provides a critique of standard cultural, philosophical and psychological notions of '**gender**' in both *Gender Trouble* and *Bodies that Matter* (1993) and argues that gender should be understood as **performativity**. In *Gender Trouble* Butler argues that '*gender* is not a noun, neither is it a set of free-floating attributes ... gender is performativity produced and compelled by the regulatory practices of gender coherence. Gender is always doing....' Furthermore, gender identity is the expression of performing gender and nothing more than this (25). Butler makes clear in her preface to *Bodies that Matter* that gender is not performed in the sense of something that is donned every morning. Gender is not intentional in that wilful sense. Gender is something that is put on a body by the materiality of its existence. One performs gender as society expects that repetitious, ritualised performance (x). In her more recent book *Undoing Gender* (2004), Butler works through the implications of her performative understanding of gender to connect them to questions of 'persistence and survival', that is human rights issues and issues of personhood as they relate to sexuality and gender, providing an analysis of intersex and transgender identity, activism, surgery and autonomy.

See **postmodern feminism; queer theory; transgenderist**

C

Canon: this term is used to denote the standard texts of a particular field. In philosophy the canon consists of the standard texts one reads in the history of philosophy, such as Plato, Descartes, Locke and Wittgenstein, and the contemporary texts that are accepted as reflecting the mainstream of philosophy. Feminists have been critical of the idea of a canon and canonical texts on a few counts. First, they view these texts as reflecting what is selected as important by mainstream philosophy and so might not represent what was historically significant. Second, in the history of philosophy, all canonical texts are written by men. Writings by women philosophers have been thoroughly excluded from the canon of philosophy. Third, the canon itself is viewed as **masculinist** and **androcentric**. This incorporates the first two problems in that what is considered significant in philosophy was determined by men and only includes men. In contemporary philosophy, women and especially feminists have a difficult time getting included in the canon. A series of texts, *Rereading the Canon*, was developed to provide a critique of the canon and to call into question the very idea of a canon. **Margaret Atherton**'s *Women Philosophers in the Early Modern Period* (1994) and Mary Ellen Waithe's series *History of Women Philosophers* (2003) both provide readings from female philosophers that have been kept out of the canon.

Card, Claudia: white US feminist philosopher specialising in social and political philosophy and lesbian theory. Claudia Card's earlier work in **lesbian ethics** represents an important contribution to feminist philosophy. Her book *Lesbian Choices* (1995) argues for the understanding of lesbian identity as an active, conscious choice in a **heteronormative** culture in which heterosexuality is very rarely a conscious choice for straight women. Her more recent work, *The Atrocity Paradigm: A Theory of Evil* (2005), charts a middle ground between the utilitarian and stoic notions of evil to analyse atrocities such as the bombings of Hiroshima, Nagasaki and Dresden, rape and sexual slavery as tools of war, and other evils such as domestic violence and incest. Card argues that feminists' attention to ending social injustices over attention to ending atrocities is mistaken. Card is also the editor of *Feminist Ethics* (1991).

Chicana Feminism and Latina Feminism: Chicanas are Mexican-American women. Latina feminism is a broader term for feminists of Spanish, Cuban, Mexican and Puerto Rican decent. Latina and Chicana feminism are theoretically aligned, sharing the same concerns, approaches and theoretical devices. **Gloria Anzaldúa**, the author of *Borderlands/La Frontera* (1987), a prominent

Chicana feminist text, describes Chicana feminism as using personal and collective narratives to theorize

> how to arrange [...] all these facets of identity: class and race and belonging to so many worlds – the Chicano world, the academic world, the world of the job, the intellectual-artistic world, the white world, being with blacks, and Natives and Asian Americans who belong to those worlds as well as popular culture. (2000: 23)

Chicana feminists exist in what Anzaldúa calls the 'borderland'. The borderland is a physical and epistemological location as well as a state of being. Anzaldúa describes the borderland as 'a vague and undetermined place created by the emotional residue of an unnatural boundary. It is in a constant state of transition. The prohibited and forbidden are its inhabitants' (1987: 24). The borderland provides Chicana feminists an important epistemological and social location from which to provide critique. They are both inside and outside of US culture and are taught to see from the perspective of someone who has been viewed as an unwanted inhabitant of US culture. She calls this position or identity the 'new mestiza consciousness', which, through straddling two cultures, works to break down **dualisms** and boundaries. Some other Chicana feminists are Cherríe Moraga and Aurora Levins Morales. **Linda Martín Alcoff,** author of *Visible Identities : Race, Gender, and the Self* (2005), is a prominent Chicana feminist philosopher. **María Lugones,** author of *Pilgrimages/Peregrinajes* (2003), is a prominent Latina feminist as is **Ofelia Schutte,** author of *Cultural Identity and Social Liberation in Latin American Thought* (1993).

Cixous, Hélène: French postmodern feminist philosopher and novelist. Cixous is an important figure in postmodern philosophy, arguing for the connection between sexuality and language. She develops and argues for feminine writing, *écriture féminine*. She first uses the term in 'The Laugh of Medusa' (1983) to indicate not only writing that is antithetical to **masculinist**, linear, representationalist writing, but to indicate the non-linear flow between writing and speech that is inherently bodily. Cixous argues that masculine writing is static, **disembodied** and free of desire. Feminine writing is where change can take place. 'Women must write her self: must write about women and bring women to writing, from which they have been driven away as violently from their own bodies . . . ' (Cixous, 1983: 279). In her essay 'Sorties' [1968] (1999) Cixous argues '[p]hallocentricism *is*. History has never produced, recorded anything but that . . . . Phallocentricism is the enemy. Of *everyone*. Men stand to lose by it, differently but as seriously as women. And it is time to transform. To invent the other history' (441). The **phallocentric** order functions through binaries. Cixous works through the binaries of western thought reflecting woman's positioning on the negative side of the binary:

Where is she?
Activity/Passivity
Sun/Moon
Culture/Nature
Day/Night
Father/Mother
Head/Heart
Intelligible/Sensitive
Logos/Pathos (440)

She argues that the position of woman as negative or other is essential to keeping the phallocentric social order running. But if women use their **otherness** against this system it would destabilise it. She writes:

> The challenging of this solidarity of logocentricism and phallocentricism has today become insistent enough – the bringing to light the fate which has been imposed upon women, of her burial – to threaten the stability of the masculine edifice which passed itself off as eternal-natural; by bringing forth from the world of femininity reflections, hypotheses which are necessarily ruinous for the bastion which still holds the authority. (441)

See **postmodern feminism**

Class: in the most straightforward sense class is where one is located on a socio-economic matrix that arises from a capitalist social structure. One's class is also thought to confer certain attributes. For example, people wrongly assume that people are poor because they are lazy and don't want to work. Class does confer certain kinds of social benefits. For example, middle-class people are more likely to be thought of as good parents and to receive social benefits based on this. Many areas of feminist philosophy provide analyses of class. Two particular areas are **Marxist feminism** and **socialist feminism**. Class is intimately tied up with **race, racism, gender** and **oppression**.
Further reading: Tong (1998)

Code, Lorraine: white Canadian feminist philosopher specialising in epistemology, ethics, philosophy of science. Code's work focuses on the intersection between ethics and epistemology. Her 1981 article 'Is the Sex of the

Knower Epistemologically Significant?' was one of the first well-recognised pieces to point to the gendered nature of knowing. Code has also made significant contributions to virtue epistemology with her arguments for epistemic responsibility. In *Epistemic Responsibility* (1987) she develops an account of epistemic responsibility in which the knower is active, situated within a context and gendered, and whose responsibilities arise out of the narrative conditions of the community in which the knower is embedded. Code extends these arguments in her 2006 book *Ecological Thinking: The Politics of Epistemic Location* by taking arguments for **situated knowledge**, the view that all knowledge comes from a particular **embodied**, located perspective, and combines them with the methodologies employed in analyses of ecology to develop **ecological thinking**. She argues for ecological thinking as a more dynamic view of situated knowledge that is a means for achieving better knowledge acquisition in medicine and the sciences. Throughout Code's work she utilises literature, legal cases, medicine, science and the everyday life to develop case examples for her arguments. Code is also the author of *What Can She Know? Feminist Theory and the Construction of Knowledge* (1991) and *Rhetorical Spaces: Essays on Gendered Locations* (1995).

See **feminist epistemology; feminist science studies; situated knowledge**

Collins, Patricia Hill: Black feminist sociologist specialising in race and gender theory and popular culture. Collins is the author of *Black Feminist Thought: Knowledge, Consciousness and the Politics of Empowerment* (1991). *Black Feminist Thought* has been groundbreaking in its systematic analysis of **race** and **gender**. In this text Collins introduces the notion of the **outsider-within** and defines **Black feminist thought**. The outsider-within is a subject position 'filled with contradictions occupied by groups with unequal power' (1998: 5). Theorising as an outsider-within 'reflects the multiplicity of being on the margins with intersecting systems of race, class, gender, sexual, and national oppression, even as such theory remains grounded in and attentive to real differences in power' (8). Black feminist thought is a type of **standpoint episte-mology** that originates from the insights of Black feminist intellectuals such as **Audre Lorde, Barbara Smith** and **bell hooks**, and the experiences of **oppression** and domination that are the legacy of slavery. It emphasises the importance of seeing Black women as **agents** of knowledge and the partiality of all knowledge. In her subsequent books, *Black Sexual Politics: African Americans, Gender, and the New Racism* (2005), *Fighting Words: Black Women and the Search for Justice* (1998) and *From Black Power to Hip Hop: Racism, Nationalism, and Feminism* (2006), she continues to critically examine the intersection of race and gender, but in these latter books there is a new attention paid to popular culture and how it replicates and fights against the 'new racism', racism that exists despite legislation that seeks to eliminate it. In *Black Sexual Politics: African Americans, Gender, and the New Racism* (2005), Collins argues that the new racism is enabled by the global economy, is transnational and thus differs from state to state, and utilises mass media to convey its hegemonic message (54). This new racism has normalised and naturalised a view of Black sexuality as animal-like and primitive, a view that becomes replicated through popular culture, is internalised by Black men and women, and constructs Black masculinity and **femininity**.

Colonisation: colonisation is the often violent, racially based system of **oppression** and domination in which land, people and ideas are occupied. The colonisation of ideas occurs through taking, using and systematising the ideas of other people and speaking authoritatively to represent those people. For example, **Chandra Talpade Mohanty** in *Feminism Without Borders: Decolonizing Theory, Practicing Solidarity* (2003) argues that white, western feminism has colonised Third World women through the 'appropriation and codification of scholarship and knowledge about women in the Third World' (17). Colonisation of the land and people occurs through the occupying, taking, using and abuse of land, resources, peoples and ways of life by an outside, usually aggressive force. Colonisation also involves the forcing of outside ideas and practices on the colonised. For example, France colonised Vietnam, used its people and resources, appropriated its ways of life and then structured Vietnamese life to model French culture through modelling French architecture, city and government structures, adopting Catholicism, the French language and French food, while at the same time exoticising and othering the Vietnamese.

See **decolonisation; other/othering; Third World feminism**

Compulsory heterosexuality: the practice of constructing heterosexual behaviour as the social norm and the only legitimate way of being. In making heterosexuality compulsory not only do we make other types of sexual lives difficult – and for some impossible – to choose, we also make culture appear to be more heterosexual than it is. Compulsory heterosexuality creates homophobia, legitimises the harm done to lesbians and gay men, and legitimises social practices, such as legislation against gay marriage, that seek to further the inequalities between straight people and lesbians, bisexuals and gay men. Many feminists have provided critiques of compulsory heterosexuality, for example **Judith Butler, Claudia Card, Marilyn Frye, Mary Daly** and **Sarah Hoagland.**

Contextual values: a term used by feminist philosopher of science **Helen Longino** in *Science as Social Knowledge* (1990) to indicate non-cognitive values, that is values that are not strictly part of practices of science but nonetheless play a role in scientific decision-making. Preferences, beliefs and cultural norms are contextual values. These include things like theory preference based on **masculinist** values or preferring a theory because the physical location in which one does research makes certain data more convincing. Contextual values play a role in scientific **objectivity.** Some feminist philosophers of science see contextual values as unavoidable, but argue that they need to be acknowledged and mitigated by a diversity of views.

See **neutrality; rationality**

D

Daly, Mary: white US feminist theologian. Daly is a one of the most well-known US feminists for several reasons. She played an early and significant role in academic feminism as well as being a public voice for **radical feminism** and for **separatism.** She has been a controversial public figure, receiving significant media coverage for having female-only upper-division feminist theory courses and tutoring male students privately. Daly's work has been influential in many areas of feminist philosophy, especially for her powerful critiques of **patriarchy.** Her earliest texts *The Church and the Second Sex* (1968) and *Beyond God the Father: Toward a Philosophy of Women's*

Liberation (1973) initiate from an existentialist perspective influenced by **Simone de Beauvoir** and argue that women's subordination and **oppression** is directly a result of the **misogyny** in Christianity. Her book *Gyn/Ecology: The Metaethics of Radical Feminism* (1978) argues that patriarchy perpetuates itself through language since language constructs reality. Thus the task of radical feminism is to construct a new language, a gynomorphic language, that displaces the language of patriarchy and to create new myths that reconstruct reality. Daly argues that feminist analysis needs 'to be free to dis-cover our own distinctions, refusing to be locked in these mental temples' (48). Among Daly's other books are *Pure Lust: Elemental Feminist Philosophy* (1984), *Outercourse: Be Dazzling Voyage* (1992) and *Quintessence ... Realizing the Archaic Future* (1999).

Decolonisation: in *Feminism Without Borders: Decolonizing Theory, Practicing Solidarity* (2003) **Chandra Talpade Mohanty** describes decolonisation as the critical, historical and collective democracy promoting process through which colonised people transform 'self, community, and governance structures' (7). It involves 'an active withdrawal of consent and resistance to structure of psychic and social domination' and results in a radical transformation of social structures and individual and collective identity (7–8). Decolonisation requires an immersion in the everyday world such that one can come to see past **hegemonic** structures and practices (254). Mohanty argues that it is essential for feminist theory because it allows individuals and collectives to critically assess and rethink 'patriarchal, heterosexual, colonial, racial and capitalist legacies' that are within feminism and leads to 'thinking through questions of resistance anchored in the daily lives of women' (8). **Ofelia Schutte** describes de-colonisation as the unhinging of 'one's identity from the inherited colonial structure' (1998: 66).

See **anti-capitalist critique; postcolonial feminism; Third World feminism**

Further reading: Schutte (1998)

Deconstruction: a method of analysis and interpretation in the poststructuralist tradition developed by French philosopher Jacques Derrida. Deconstruction argues that the understanding of any text, be it an actual written text or text understood more broadly to include truth claims, social values, norms and practices, is inherently incomplete because all texts are interpreted by those coming out of complex social structures and histories. Because of this complexity, texts are claimed to have a multiplicity of voices contained within them as well as no one unitary, coherent interpretation. Deconstruction has been important for several areas of feminist thought such as **feminist postmodernism**. For example **Judith Butler** conceives of the body as a text in order to consider how gender is an act of **performativity**. It has also been influential in some areas of feminist thought in which it might be less obvious. For example, in **feminist science studies, Sandra Harding** considers how scientific knowledge is a construction of particular societies and is inherently incomplete.

Further reading: Butler (1993); Derrida (1967)

Différance: Deconstructionist Jacques Derrida first used the term in his *De la Grammatolgie* (1967) to describe the condition necessary for thought and language, differing/deferring. Differing differentiates signs/words and thus things from each other. Deferring marks the means by which signs/words refer to each other. There is a gap that exists in that signs/language are always needed to describe signs/words and thus can never fully get at what they mean. We are always trapped within language and are constantly postponing or deferring meaning. Thus language is inadequate to describe reality. **Postmodern feminists** used Derrida's *différance* to describe the state of 'woman, the other, the feminine [as] left unthematized and silent in the void between language and reality' (Tong 1998). For example, **Hélène Cixous** asks

> I write 'mother.' What is the connection between mother and women, daughter? I write 'woman.' What is the difference? This is what my body teaches me: first of all be wary of names, they are nothing but social tools, rigid concepts, little cages of meaning to keep us from getting mixed up with each other, without which the Society of Capitalist Siphoning would collapse. (1991: 49)

Diffraction: Donna Haraway (1997) develops diffraction in reaction to standard conceptions of **reflexivity**. She worries that because standard notions of reflexivity assume that one can recognise and identify one's own cultural biases, one supposes a transparency of self that does not exist. This moves the problem of reflexivity farther back because in Haraway's view there is no original transparent self to be found and known upon which one can readily measure and identify one's biases. Like two mirrors reflecting infinitely, reflexivity sets up a continual pattern of reflection that stretches back without ever encountering the 'real' image. Haraway argues that diffraction does not search for an authentic self, but understands the self and its history to be heterogeneous. Diffraction is a new critical consciousness that is a technology in itself and is an active, critical practice that subjects the ways we generate knowledge to analysis and change. Diffraction is a process in which actors in technoscience and in the study of technoscience take responsibility for their physical and language practices, recognising that responsibility 'requires an immersion in worldly-material semiotic practices, where the analysts, as well as the humans and nonhumans studied, are all at risk – morally, politically, technically, and epistemologically' (1997: 190). This risk involves potentially destabilising previously held commitments, beliefs and values and the floundering involved in seeking to replace these with 'better' commitments.

See **strong/strategic reflexivity**

Further reading: Haraway (1991, 1997); Harding (1991, 1998)

Disability Studies: disability is a type of **oppression** that results from society being inadequately equipped to deal with the different needs of people with impairments (Thomas, 2002). Disability studies is a critical approach to this social oppression. Members of the disability studies community have faulted feminists for their lack of interest in disability as a type of oppression in need of feminist insight, but since the mid-1990s there has been an increased attention in the feminist community to disability. Rosemarie Garland-Thomson argues that feminist theory has 'insights, methods, and perspectives that would deepen disability studies' and that feminists fail to recognise disability as a difference that affects women (1996: 73). They have not noticed how disability is linked to 'reproductive technology, the place of bodily difference, the particularities of oppression, the ethics of care, the construction of the subject' (74). In *The Rejected Body* (1996) Susan Wendell argues that feminist theory needs to take disability seriously as a type of difference. She asks:

What would it mean ... to value disabilities as differences? It would certainly mean not assuming that every disability is a tragic loss or that everyone with a disability wants to be 'cured.' It would mean seeking out and respecting the knowledge and perspectives of people with disabilities. It would mean being willing to learn about and respect ways of being and forms of consciousness that are unfamiliar. And it would mean giving up the myths of control and quest for perfection of the human body. (84)

Theorising about the intersection of gender and disability has become an increasingly important part of feminist theory. See, for example, *Foucault and the Government of Disability* by Shelley Tremain (2005) and *Disability, Difference, Discrimination* by **Anita Silvers**, David Wasserman and **Mary Mahowald** (1998).

Disembodied: some feminists argue that the history of western philosophy has assumed and privileged a disembodied knower, in other words a thinker that is free from the biases of a body. Many argue that this arises from Cartesian mind–body **dualism**, which became the foundation for the rest of modern philosophy. Because the mind was privileged over the body and the body was seen to lead the body astray in Cartesianism, the best epistemic strategy was to rid the mind of the body's influence. Some feminists, for example **Susan Bordo** in her book *Flight to Objectivity* (1987), argue that the history of western philosophy since the modern period (sixteenth century and onward) has been a project of disembodiment. Furthermore, some feminists argue that the mistake philosophy has made is thinking that it can rid the mind of the body's influence. Wrapped up in this distancing from the body is that in much of the history of western philosophy women are viewed to be more tied to the body than men and therefore cannot be disembodied or real knowers in philosophy. Thus, according to this view, women couldn't be real philosophers. Some feminist philosophers have argued for a more embodied philosophy.

See **embodiment**

Further reading: Grosz (1994b); Weiss (1999)

Disorder of Sexual Development (DSD)/Intersex: the Intersex Society of North America (ISNA) characterises intersex/ DSD as a term used to describe a set of physical conditions 'in which a person is born with reproductive or sexual anatomy that doesn't seem to fit the typical definitions of female or male' (www.isna.org). Some of these conditions are diagnosed at birth, others later in life. Because people with intersex conditions challenge social norms regarding sex and gender, the physical conditions of intersex are frequently managed medically through surgery and hormonal treatment as well as socially through behavioural training. Thus the medical community and some parents work at reinforcing not just behavioural gender norms, but the expectations of genital difference through surgery so that the essential congruity between sex and gender and the expectations of sexual dimorphism are replicated.

Anne Fausto-Sterling in *Sexing the Body* (2000) describes the history of the treatment of people with intersexed conditions as a 'most literal tale of social construction – the story of the emergence of strict surgical enforcement of a two-party system of sex ...' (32). She argues that intersex conditions necessarily challenge the notion that **sex** is fixed and biological and **gender** is purely a social construct and seeks a more dynamic view of sex and gender, one that will not be so destructive of the lives of those with intersexed conditions.

Recently intersex activists have come to prefer the term Disorder of Sexual Development because it allows them to work more fruitfully with the medical community. According to Sherri Groveman Morris in 'DSD But Intersex Too: Shifting Paradigms Without Abandoning Roots' (2006), '[p]rior to the adoption of "DSD" as the preferred term, there was apparently some confusion about whether certain medical conditions properly fell under the heading of "intersex." ISNA's avowed aim in preferring "DSD" is to support improved medical care for children born with such conditions' (1).

See **Butler, Judith; essentialism; social construction**
Further reading: Butler (2004)

Dualistic/dualism: dualistic thinking is a method of thinking in binaries such as mind/body, culture/nature, sex/gender, male/female, objectivity/subjectivity in which each term is seen to be mutually exclusive. Dualistic thinking tends to privilege one half of the binary over the other. Some feminists have argued that such a privileging arises out of the modern period and that this privileging is **masculinist**. They have also argued that it is socially, ethically and epistemically dangerous because some groups, such as all women, the poor and people of colour, become equated with the negative half of the dualism where as white men, especially socially advantaged white men, are equated with the positive half of the dualism. Thus white men are seen to be objective, whereas a woman of colour is seen to be incapable of objectivity and is thus subjective and not a proper ethical or epistemic agent.

Karen Warren in *Ecofeminist Philosophy* (2000) points to prevailing dualisms in western philosophy as a source of conceptual and practical domination. Man/woman, culture/nature, mind/body, reason/emotion exist as hierarchical dualisms in western thought with man, culture, mind and reason having higher value than women, nature, body and emotion. This conceptual dualism leads to the practical outcome of the valued half of the dualism having 'power over' the devalued half and thus the 'twin' domination of women and nature.

Cixous in 'Sorties' [1986] (1999) works through the binaries of western thought reflecting woman's positioning on the negative side of the binary:

> Where is she?
> Activity/Passivity
> Sun/Moon
> Culture/Nature
> Day/Night
> Father/Mother
> Head/Heart
> Intelligible/Sensitive
> Logos/Pathos (440)

Like Warren she points to women and femininity always being on the negative side of the binary, thus mirroring their social status.

E

Ecofeminism: the term ecofeminism was first used by French feminist philosopher Françoise d'Eaubonne in her book *Le féminisme ou la mort* (1976) (Tong, 1998). D'Eaubonne argued that a balanced relationship with the environment and the end of **patriarchy** are intimately linked. She critically links population growth and degradation of the environment with patriarchy's view of women as merely reproductive bodies. She further connects this to patriarchal capitalism's ('Daddy's') need for soldiers (Warren, 2000). Rosemary Ruether in her 1975 book *New Women/New Earth* preceded d'Eaubonne's terminology, ideologically arguing that there is no possibility of liberation for women without a 'radical reshaping' of our treatment of the environment (204). Some ecofeminists have argued that women have a stronger physical, emotional and spiritual connection to nature and thus are most suited to ethical interactions with the environment (Spretnak, 1982). Other ecofeminists have focused on the social construction of gender and nature that leads to women's and nature's subordination (Merchant, 1980).

Like most areas of feminist philosophy, ecofeminism is pluralist in its approaches, though there are ideological connections. **Karen Warren** in *Ecofeminist Philosophy* (2000) argues that '[e]cological feminists ("ecofeminists") claim that there are important connections between the unjustified dominations of women, people of color, children, and the poor and the unjustified domination of nature' (1). Warren points to many connections between the domination of women and nature that have been cited by ecofeminists. For example, she points to prevailing **dualisms** in western philosophy as a source of conceptual and practical domination. Man/woman, culture/nature, mind/body, reason/emotion exist as hierarchical dualisms in western thought with man, culture, mind and reason having higher value than women, nature, body and emotion. This conceptual dualism leads to the practical outcome of the valued half of the dualism having 'power over' the devalued half and thus the 'twin' domination of women and nature (2000). **Val Plumwood,** in *Environmental Culture: The Ecological Crisis of Reason* (2002), argues that western culture's obsession is not only irrational, but what masquerades as rationality is irrational and has led to our current ecological and social crisis. She claims that the 'ecological crisis is the crisis of a cultural "mind" that cannot acknowledge and adapt itself properly to its material "body", the embodied and ecological support base it draws on in the long-denied counter-sphere of "nature"' (15).

Ecological Thinking: Canadian philosopher **Lorraine Code** (2006) takes arguments for **situated knowledge,** the view that all knowledge comes from a particular **embodied,** located perspective, and combines them with the methodologies employed in analyses of ecology to develop ecological thinking. Code argues for 'ecological thinking' as a more dynamic view of situated knowledge that is a means for achieving better knowledge acquisition in medicine and the sciences. Ecological thinking views situation as a place from which to know and a place to know or to interrogate to understand how that location enables or disables the ability to know. Thus not only does knowledge come from a more critical perspective, but is also knowledge that interrogates that perspective. Ecological thinking seeks to understand the differences between particular epistemic locations and seeks to negotiate differences within these locations. According to Code, ecological thinking is also more sympathetic to the natural and social sciences, yet is still critical of the sciences as the ultimate epistemological authority.

See **Haraway, Donna**

Ecriture féminine: *écriture féminine* is literally translated from French as the 'writings of women' or 'women's writing'. In as much as women are viewed as bodily, it is sometimes translated as 'writing from the body' and expresses a 'women-centered theoretical position' (Penrod, 1996: 25). *Ecriture féminine* is a label applied to the work of some French feminists, among them are **Luce Irigaray, Julia Kristeva** and **Hélène Cixous.** Cixous first uses the term in 'The Laugh of Medusa' (1975/1983) to indicate not only writing that is antithetical to **masculinist**, linear, representationalist writing, but to indicate the non-linear flow between writing and speech that is inherently bodily. Cixous argues that masculine writing is static, **disembodied** and free of desire. Feminine writing is where change can take place. 'Women must write her self: must write about women and bring women to writing, from which they have been driven away as violently from their own bodies . . .' (Cixous, 1983: 279).

Embodiment/embodied: embodiment indicates the experience of being in the world as lived, enculturated beings. It is a non-dualistic way of thinking about the body and humanness, starting from the perspective that is there is no separation of mind and body. Furthermore, thinking and theorising about ourselves as embodied means we think and experience through raced, classed, gendered, abled in different ways and aged bodies. We intersect with culture through these facets of embodiment. Theorising about and through embodiment is a recent philosophical approach. The history of western philosophy has taken a decidedly **disembodied** approach. It has not only consistently prioritised the mind over the body, it has viewed the body as a detriment to the mind and rational thinking and viewed the body as mechanical and/or animal-like. Maurice Merleau-Ponty, a continental philosopher, and John Dewey, a pragmatist philosopher, are both twentieth-century philosophers who did theorise about the body, but they did so from a genderless, raceless and classless perspective. One of the important insights of feminist theory is that thinking from an embodied perspective and through embodiment provides a better understanding of ourselves in the world. For example, **Susan Bordo** in her book *Unbearable Weight* (1993) uses the lens of the gendered body to understand how advertising, media and cultural norms have taught women how to see their bodies. She states that 'culture – working not only through ideology and images, but through the organization of the family, the construction of personality, the training of perceptions – as not singularly contributory but *productive* of eating disorders' (50).

See **dualism**

Further reading: Weiss (1999)

Epistemology of Ignorance: philosopher Charles Mills coins the term 'epistemology of ignorance' in his 1999 book *The Racial Contract*. He argues that under the terms of the Racial Contract, which is a subtext of the social contract, whites agree to misinterpret the world. The racial contract is an agreement to be ignorant of or to misinterpret the conditions of society and the privileges whites experience. This agreement is held in place by the assurance that this misinterpretation will count as true by those that benefit and maintain this wilful ignorance, whites. Mills tells us that this ignorance is an inverted epistemology. Ignorance is experienced as knowledge because it provides a worldview that is cohesive with whites' expectations of what the world is like. The term has become important recently in feminist theory. Feminists such as **Nancy Tuana** have adopted his terminology to talk about knowledge that is intentionally left out of scientific and social knowledge about women and other cultures. Ignorance and its epistemological and ethical significance have been the subject of several important feminist texts across feminist philosophy. For example, **Marilyn Frye** in her essay 'On Being White' (in Frye, 1983) argues that ignorance is frequently wilful. **Luce Irigaray** in *This Sex Which Is Not One* (1985a) argues that ignorance is actively constructed around women's sexuality.

Essentialism: the view that an object has an essence that defines, makes or determines what that entity is. Essences are taken to be fixed and unchanging, the 'thatness' of something. Culture, experience, history are taken to have no bearing on essences. In the history of philosophy everything from justice and beauty to sex and human nature are taken to have essences. Feminist philosophy has raised numerous objections against essentialism. By and large to argue that someone or something is an essentialist is to make a critical comment that they are not recognising the cultural particularity of something. For example, philosophers who hold that homosexuality is a fixed category may have pointed out to them that though there have been same-sex sexual and loving relationships throughout history, not all cultures view this activity in the same sense or in a negative sense as contemporary western culture indicates when something or someone is labelled homosexual. Philosophers may point to socially acceptable relations among men and boys during the Roman Empire that were a means of education and social mobility or may point to loving and socially sanctioned relationships among Elizabethan women as activities that do have a very different meaning than what western culture labels homosexual.

A feminist to provide one of the earliest critiques of essentialism is **Simone de Beauvoir** (1952) in *The Second Sex* in which she critiques gender essentialism, arguing that existence precedes essence. By this she means that in virtue of something existing within a culture it is given by that culture an essence. The essence itself is not some fixed presocial given but is generated by that culture. Thus an essence is not an essence at all in the sense that it is defined by philosophy. Some feminists have been critical of essentialism because they believe it leads to *sexism*, **racism** and monolithic views of beauty, justice and truth. They also have argued that essentialism is entwined with numerous power structures that are oppressive to all women and all marginalised groups.

Some feminists have employed what they called **strategic essentialism**. Strategic essentialism is a concept used first by **Gayatri Chakravorty Spivak** in her essays 'Can the Subaltern Speak?' (1988) and 'Subaltern Studies: Deconstructing Historiography' [1985] (1995) to indicate a political and temporary use of **essentialism** for the subversive ends of creating or understanding a group self-consciousness. Spivak, in her critique of the Subaltern Studies group, a working group of **postcolonial theorists**, argues that when she reads their work 'from within but against the grain' (1985: 214) she reads the project as an attempt to develop a narrow consciousness, a self-consciousness, that would allow the employment and deployment of a strategic essentialism to understand the **subaltern** woman. Spivak makes clear that strategic essentialism is not a 'search for lost origins' (1988: 295) that locates a static historical subject, but a critical, temporary method of locating self-consciousness for strategic ends. **Luce Irigaray** also develops a type of strategic essentialism in *This Sex Which Is Not One* (1985a). She uses the term mimicry or *mimétisme* to describe a type of oppositional discourse in which women assume the characteristics assigned to them by **phallocentric** culture in order to challenge phallocentrism and its description of and prescription for women. An example of this would be women employing a feminine style of writing, *écriture féminine* to argue against male stereotypes of women. Strategic essentialism has been used in many areas of feminist philosophy, including but not limited to **postcolonial feminist theory, Chicana feminism and Latina feminism, feminist science studies** and **queer theory**.

Ethics of Care: psychologist **Carol Gilligan** put forth ethics of care as an alternative to hierarchal, principled approaches to ethics in her book *In a Different Voice* (1982). Gilligan, through her empirical research, argued against the empirical work of moral psychologist Lawrence Kohlberg who asserted that in general girls and therefore women did not morally develop to the highest principled levels while boys and men were more likely to develop a principled approach. Gilligan presented an alternative empirical account that showed that girls and women approached ethical situations differently than men, through connectedness and the primacy of caring relationships, instead of through abstract principles that are the foundation for an ethics of justice. It is a view in which 'relationships between persons, rather than individual rights or individual preferences, are a primary focus' (Held, 2002: 31). Feminist philosophers such as **Nel Noddings**, **Eva Kittay** and **Virginia Held** have provided philosophical support for Gilligan's empirical work, arguing for the important moral values ensconced within caring for those dependent upon another, and have extended her arguments to many applied areas of feminist theory. Noddings extends her insights to education; Kittay extends hers to dependency relationships and gendered work, and Held extends her views to women's labour and the market. Gilligan's work and ethics of care renewed substantial interested in **feminist ethics** as well as initiating the serious study of women and girls as moral **agents**.

Further reading: Held (2005); Kittay (1999); Noddings (2003)

Eurocentric: the view that most if not all essential knowledge, ethics and culture originated in Europe and the US. Implicit in this is that other types of knowledge and culture are not as legitimate or significant as European. Eurocentrism is sometimes held as an overt belief, but it frequently functions as a **background assumption** that leads to biased decision-making and harm to others. An example of Eurocentrism is the view that all philosophy originated in European culture. This view neglects to acknowledge that many other cultures have rich philosophical traditions and that some of our philosophical traditions are borrowed from or influenced by other cultures. For example, many argue that ancient philosophy was influenced by Egyptian philosophy and that medieval philosophy was influenced by Islamic philosophy.

F

Femininity: femininity is a set of socially constructed characteristics applied to women. Among these characteristics are nurturing, emotional, irrational, subjective, passivity, dependency, **other**. There have been numerous feminist analyses of femininity. **Hélène Cixous** in 'Sorties' [1986] (1999) illustrates how the prevailing dualisms place women on the negative side of the binaries. She says:

> Where is she?
> Activity/Passivity
> Sun/Moon
> Culture/Nature
> Day/Night
> Father/Mother
> Head/Heart
> Intelligible/Sensitive
> Logos/Pathos (440)

Sandra Bartky in *Femininity and Domination* (1991) points out that when women engage in activities that are regarded as independent or self-beneficial, they are seen as denying or negating their femininity. **Iris Marion Young** in 'Throwing Like a Girl' (1980) argues that the **hegemonic** norms of femininity are used to keep women from reaching their full potential. Women learn to conceive of their bodies as soft, passive, unathletic, and learn to comport themselves and carry their bodies to mimic this cultural norm. **Sarah Hoagland** (1994) agues that femininity 'normalizes male domination and paints a portrait of women as subordinate and naively content with being controlled' (460).

See **gender and sex; masculinist**

Feminist Aesthetics: a pluralistic area of study that uses feminism as a lens to analyse art, literature, architecture, music, dance, the human body, fashion and culture as well as to question theories, aesthetic categories and aesthetic approaches regarding these areas. Feminist approaches in aesthetics have questioned the objectifying of women's bodies through art, have analysed how culture forms conceptions of high and low art, beauty and aesthetic value, and have provided critical analyses of popular culture and how it constructs gender, as well as architecture and food. Feminist aesthetics has also generated new approaches to art such that artists are producing explicitly feminist work that calls into question such things as the primacy of the male artist, the objectified female body and **essentialism** in art and aesthetics.

See **Grosz, Elizabeth; Probyn, Elspeth**

Further reading: Brand and Korsmeyer (1995); Korsmeyer (2004)

Feminist Empiricism: a type of **feminist epistemology** that views the methodologies and values of science as the best way to eradicate **masculinist** and **Eurocentric** values from science and to promote **objectivity**. **Sandra Harding** in *Whose Science? Whose Knowledge?* (1991) lists some of the virtues of feminist empiricism. Among the virtues of feminist empiricism are the following:

1. By challenging incomplete applications of scientific method and not the idea of scientific method, it accords well with what we know about science. It thus preserves scientific methodology.
2. Since it doesn't challenge the overall values of science or scientific method it is amenable to many of those that might normally be hostile to feminist critiques of science.

Feminist empiricists argue that scientific method on its own is not enough to eliminate **androcentric** biases in science if feminist concerns are not taken into account. Harding points out that feminist empiricists also think that alternative approaches need to be employed in the natural and social sciences that question mainstream research practices and modes of inquiry. **Helen Longino** is a well-known feminist empiricist.

See **feminist epistemology; feminist science studies**
Further reading: Longino (1990, 2002)

Feminist Epistemologies: a diverse group of theories of knowledge that tend to question the standard S knows that P epistemologies of mainstream philosophy. Feminist epistemologies arose in response to the feminist analysis that standard epistemology may not only not capture all there is to knowledge and knowledge acquisition, but that the very underpinnings and methodologies of mainstream epistemology may be sexist and **masculinist**.

Feminist epistemologies tend to be critical of mainstream epistemology and work to develop alternative epistemological frameworks. Among this diverse group of epistemologies are **feminist standpoint theory, feminist empiricism, situated knowledge** and **ecological thinking** as well as feminist reinterpretations of naturalism and coherence theory.

Further reading: Alcoff and Potter (1993)

Feminist Ethics: a pluralistic area of study that seeks to insert itself into the mainstream discussion of ethical theory which has been largely **androcentric** and thus overlooks women and gender in the formulation of ethics and social theory. It also seeks to question the very foundation of mainstream ethical and social theory. Feminist ethicists critique a variety of positions that are subjects of mainstream ethical theory such as views of justice, moral agency, universal ethical claims, **rationality** as the only basis for ethical judgement, and moral autonomy. They forge new ethical approaches such as **lesbian ethics, ethics of care,** maternal ethics, **ecofeminism,** racial justice and **disability studies** and take on such subjects as **reproductive rights, reproductive technologies,** poverty, sexual violence, pornography and **heterosexism.**

Further reading: Card (1991); Lindemann (2005)

Feminist Science Studies: a diverse area of study that includes feminists in sociology of science, anthropology of science, history of science, philosophy of science as well as practising scientists. Members of the feminist science studies community approach their analysis of the natural and social sciences in a plurality of ways. What ties all of these approaches together is the commitment to providing a critical analysis of scientific practice that takes gender into account. Some of the ways this is done consist of: looking into the history of science to recover women scientists or to study the role women had in the history of science; considering what kinds of questions science might ask if more women were included in scientific practice; looking for **androcentric** and **masculinist** biases in scientific theories or practices; questioning the very endeavour of science; questioning the **objectivity** and neutrality in the sciences.

See **ecological thinking; feminist empiricism; situated knowledge**

Further reading: Mayberry (2001); Tuana (1989)

Firestone, Shulamith: white, Jewish, Canadian **radical feminist** and activist living in the US. Firestone is recognised for her book *The Dialectic of Sex* (1970), written during the height of **second wave feminism,** in which she employs **Marxist feminism** and reworks **Simone de Beauvoir's** explanations of woman's subordinate position. Firestone argues that it is not the means of production that oppress women, but the means of reproduction that do so. In other words, women, by their very biology as reproducers, are oppressed. This oppression leads to what she calls 'sex class'. Thus, instead of pointing to the social construction of the family, Firestone points to the biological construction of the family. She says 'the natural reproductive difference between the sexes led directly to the first division of labour at the origins of class, as well as furnishing the paradigm for caste (discrimination based on biological characteristics)' (9). Sex class set up the conditions for all types of **oppression**.

To end their subordination women must seize the means of reproduction. They therefore must take over and employ **reproductive technologies,** and use these technologies to their advantage to free themselves of gender subordination. In Firestone's words:

> Their seizure of the means of *production*, so as to assure the elimination of sexual classes requires the revolt of the underclass (women) and the seizure of control of *reproduction*: not only the full restoration to women of ownership of their own bodies, but also their (temporary) seizure of control of human fertility – the new biology as well as all the social institutions of child-bearing and child-rearing. (11)

Once women are freed from the burden of bearing children there will be no reason for the gender roles that lead to the subordination of women. This will generate an androgynous existence for men and women that will be the result of the 'reintegration of the Male (Technological Mode) with the Female (Aesthetic Mode)' (174), leading to what Firestone calls an 'all-encompassing culture' and eventually a full cultural revolution.

First Wave Feminism: a term that came into use in the late 1960s feminist movement (the second wave) to refer to activist women in the UK and US during the mid-nineteenth and early twentieth centuries who were seeking the right for women to vote, to higher education, to birth control, to employment rights, to married women's property rights and to equitable marriage laws. First wave feminists in the US and UK did not refer to themselves as 'feminists'. The term was not widely adopted until second wave feminism. First wave feminists by and large were focused on the needs of middle-class educated women. The needs of white working-class and poor women went largely unrecognised by both the UK and US movements, as did the needs of women of colour. Well-known women in the UK first wave feminist movement are Barbara Bodichon and Bessie Rayner Parkes. Susan B. Anthony, Elizabeth Cady Stanton, Alice Paul, Matilda Joslyn Gage and Jane Adams are well-recognised names from the US first wave movement.

Further reading: Banks (1987)

Fraser, Nancy: white US social and political philosopher. Fraser, in her 1996 book *Justice Interruptus: Critical Reflections on the 'Postsocialist' Condition,* analyses the 'postsocialist' condition, which she describes as 'a skeptical mood or structure of feeling that marks the post-1989 state of the Left. [It] expresses authentic doubts bound to genuine opacities concerning the historical possibilities for social change' (3). Fraser argues the postsocialist condition sets up a series of either/or dichotomies that appear to be mutually exclusive, such as 'class politics or identity politics? Social politics or cultural politics? Equality or difference? Redistribution or recognition?' (4). In order for significant social change to take place and for injustices to be remedied these must not be seen as either/or categories, but must be integrated as approaches for creating change. Fraser continues this line of thinking in her unique text *Redistribution or Recognition? A Political-Philosophical Exchange* (2003), which is a philosophical conversation with German political theorist Axel Honnet.

Frye, Marilyn: white US feminist philosopher specialising in metaphysics and philosophy of language. Frye writes from an intentional antiracist, lesbian perspective in two books, *The Politics of Reality: Essays in Feminist Theory* (1983) and *The Willful Virgin: Essays in Feminism, 1976–1992* (1992). These texts provide critical analyses of **whiteness, heteronormativity** and **patriarchy**, as well as arguments for the visibility of lesbian identity and **separatism**. Her essay 'On Being White: Toward a Feminist Understanding of Race and White Supremacy' in *The Politics of Reality* seeks to work through the white privilege of academic feminism as well as white privilege in US culture. Frye argues that whites actively practise ignorance of other cultures and this active ignorance is a privilege of whiteness – whites can choose to ignore the lives and experiences of others.

In her essay 'In and Out of Harm's Way: Arrogance and Love' in *The Politics of Reality* (1983) Frye provides an account of **patriarchy** in which she distinguishes between the arrogant eye and the loving eye. The arrogant eye, intrinsic to patriarchy, allows men to 'organize everything with reference to themselves and their own interests' (67). It also allows men to coerce women into a narrow range of options, yet satisfies patriarchy's ideology of freedom and choice. Thus in **phallocratic** reality men can see choice when none really exists. In contrast, the loving eye does not subsume the other under her reality. It recognises the separateness and independence of the one loved. The loving eye is attentive, listening and questioning (75). Frye questions what it would mean not to be moulded by the arrogant eye, but to be seen through the loving eye. She argues that through the loving eye woman can begin to interpret her own experience and world outside of the vision of patriarchy. Frye's essay 'Oppression' in *The Politics of Reality* (1983) develops her now well-known analogy of the birdcage to describe the experience of **oppression**. Frye argues that if you look at each individual wire of a bird cage you cannot see why the bird doesn't just fly around it, but if you look at the whole cage it is 'perfectly obvious that the bird is surrounded by a network of systematically related barriers, no one of which would be the least hindrance to its flight, but which, by their relations to each other, are as confining as the solid walls of a dungeon' (5). Like the birdcage, oppression is a system of interconnected barriers whose power can only be understood by seeing the connections and how they function together to diminish, impede, weaken, **marginalise** and confine one's daily life.

G

Gatens, Moira: white Australian feminist philosopher specialising in history of philosophy and social and political philosophy. Gatens is part of a growing group of feminists interested in philosophy of the body. In her book *Imaginary Bodies: Ethics, Power, Corporeality* (1995) Gatens develops an understanding of cultural bodily representations as imaginaries, 'those ready-made images and symbols through which we make sense of social bodies and which determine, in part, their value, their status and what will be deemed their appropriate treatment' (viii). She views social imaginaries of the body to be multiple and historically situated. Gatens extends her argument to the 'body politic' arguing that it shares characteristics with the masculine imaginary body. She uses this to explain women's subordinate social and legal status. Gatens is also the co-author with **Genevieve Lloyd** of *Collective Imaginings: Spinoza, Past and Present* (1999b), co-editor of *Australian Feminism: A Companion* (1999a), the author of *Feminism and Philosophy: Perspectives on Difference and Equality* (1991).

Gender and Sex: in the 1970s second wave feminists along with sexologists argued that sex and gender are distinct from each other. They argued that gender is the result of social institutions and is a learned behaviour, where as sex was a biological category. Thus gender is a social construction and a product of nurturing, while sex is a fixed biological given and a product of nature. Feminist biologist Anne Fausto-Sterling recounts the history of the term in the following way:

> Feminists argued that although men's and women's bodies serve different reproductive functions, few other sex differences come with the territory, unchangeable by life's vicissitudes. If girls couldn't learn math as easily, the problem wasn't built into their brains. The difficulty resulted from gender norms – different expectations and opportunities for boys and girls. Having a penis, rather than a vagina is a sex difference. Boys performing better than girls on math exams is a gender difference. (2000: 4)

Traits like nurturing, connectedness, aggression, linear thinking, activity and passivity have been described as purely the result of gender. Physical attributes like breasts, vaginas, labia, estrogen, testosterone, penises, testicles, semen and reproductive capacities have been labelled sex. Since the 1990s some thinkers have begun to problematise the sex/gender distinction. Tom Laqueur in *Making Sex* (1992) argues that prior to the late nineteenth century western thinking employed a one sex model, a model that viewed women's reproductive organs as inverted, inferior forms of male reproductive organs. There were two genders, but one sex, according to Laqueur. **Elizabeth Grosz** in 'Experimental Desire: Rethinking Queer Subjectivity' (1994a) argues that in thinking about sex and gender theorists should not only focus on the instability of gender, but should 'focus on the instabilities of sex itself, of bodies themselves' (140). Thus both Grosz and Laqueur argue sex itself, like gender, is a social construction. Anne Fausto-Sterling in *Sexing the Body* (2000) argues that scientists create truths about sex and **sexuality** that become **embodied**. We come to see our bodies as sexed in the way that scientists construct our sex and sexuality. Furthermore, behaviours that we take to be gendered and purely social are connected to sexed bodies. These need to be understood together 'as part of a developmental system' (246). Thus Fausto-Sterling argues that we can see sex and gender as both being products of nurture and nature and must work to understand them together.

See **femininity**; **heteronormative**

Gilligan, Carol: white US feminist psychologist. Gilligan put forth **ethics of care** as an alternative to hierarchal, principled approaches to ethics in her book *In a Different Voice: Psychological Theory and Women's Development* (1982). Gilligan, through her empirical research, argued against the empirical work of moral psychologist Lawrence Kohlberg who asserted that in general girls and therefore women did not morally develop to the highest principled levels while boys and men did. Gilligan presented an alternative empirical account that showed that girls and women approached ethical situations differently than men, through connectedness and the primacy of caring relationships instead of through abstract principles that are the foundation for an ethics of justice. It is a view in which 'relationships between persons, rather than individual rights or individual preferences, are a primary focus' (Held, 2002: 31). Gilligan's work generated substantial interest in the feminist community in **feminist ethics**, with numerous theorists utilising her research. Gilligan's other books include *Women, Girls, and*

Psychotherapy: Reframing Resistance (1991) and *The Birth of Pleasure* (2003).
See **Held, Virginia; Kittay, Eva; Noddings, Nel**

Globalisation: it could be argued that in the twenty-first century globalisation is women's biggest threat and should be a cause against which all feminists unite. Not only does globalisation disproportionately affect women, it disproportionately affects Third World women, all women of colour regardless of nationality, and all women living in poverty regardless of nationality and race. In *Feminism Without Borders* (2003) **Chandra Talpade Mohanty** defines globalisation as

> the production of an epoch of 'borderlessness.' The mobility, and borderlessness, of technology (e.g., the Internet), financial capital, environmental wastes, modes of governance (e.g., the World Trade Organization), as well as cross-national political movements (e.g., struggles against the World Bank and the International Monetary Fund) characterizes globalisation at the beginning of the twenty-first century. (172)

In *Water Wars: Privatization, Pollution, and Profit* (2002) **Vandana Shiva** describes globalisation as a double fascism in which exists 'the economic fascism that destroys people's rights to resources and the fundamentalist fascism that feeds on people's displacement, dispossession, economic insecurities, and fears' (xii). Thus, for Shiva, not only do people lose their access to resource rights, such as water, land, agricultural and community resources, including the knowledge generated by communities, the growth of religious fundamentalism is also fuelled by the effects of globalisation.

Globalisation and the oppression of women are inextricably tied together through poverty, unrecognised labour, sex trafficking of women and children, and lack of women in critical positions to create change. In 2002 70 per cent of the world's poor were women. Eighty per cent of displaced people from the Third World are women (Mohanty, 2003: 234). Exporting women's labour is a result of globalisation. One area in which this is readily seen is the exporting of women to work as foreign maids. In 2002 approximately 1.5 million women were exported to work as foreign maids (Seager, 2003: 72). In the US 47 per cent of women are among the lowest wage earners (Seager, 2003: 62). Globally what counts as work is still frequently not the kind of work women do (for example, domestic work, childcare, small-scale farming, crafts), thus accounting for women's labour is challenging. Sex trade has proliferated through globalisation as poverty deepens in some countries and wealth increases in others; women's and girls' bodies become a commodity for the poor to sell and the rich to buy. In 2002 a minimum estimate of women and children trafficked out of South East Asia is 225,000 and out of South Asia is 150,000 (Seager, 2003: 57). The International Monetary Fund has no women on its board of directors and only 2 per cent of International Monetary Fund governors are women. Women account for only 8 per cent of the World Bank directors and only 6 per cent of the World Bank governors (Seager, 2003: 88). Globalisation has led to a redefinition of humans as both commodities and consumers and 'global markets replace the commitments to economic, sexual, and racial equality' (Mohanty, 2003: 235).

Because globalisation, capitalism and gender oppression are mutually reinforcing, Mohanty argues that **anti-capitalist** and **transnational feminist** struggles must work to resist and re-envision a new world democracy, one that attends to the particular needs of particular women. She says:

> It is especially on the bodies and lives of women and girls from the Third World/South – the Two-Thirds World – that global capitalism writes its script, and it is by paying attention to and theorising the experiences of these communities of women and girls that we demystify capitalism as a system of debilitating sexism and racism and envision anticapitalist resistance. Thus, any analysis of the effects of globalisation needs to centralize the experiences and struggles of these particular communities of women and girls. (235)

Furthermore, Mohanty, Shiva and numerous other feminists, especially Third World feminists and feminist of colour, have argued that fighting globalisation, in other words an antiglobalisation movement, needs to be a central project of all of feminist theory, not just the responsibility of Third World/Two-Thirds World women, who have already been engaged in this struggle for years.

Grosz, Elizabeth: white Australian feminist philosopher teaching in the US, specialising in philosophy of the body, space and becoming. Grosz is a leading theorist in **embodiment**. What makes her contribution to this area unique is the perspectives from which she approaches embodiment – space, time, biology. In her book *Volatile Bodies: Toward a Corporeal Feminism* (1994b) she puts the body at the centre of her analysis instead of using it instrumentally to help understand subjectivity. For Grosz the body *is* subjectivity. Grosz argues that bodies are 'not inert; they function interactively and productively. They act and react. They generate what is new, surprising, unpredictable' (xi). As cultural objects bodies are rewritten thus also rewriting the body's biology. Her book *Nick of Time: Politics, Evolution, and the Untimely* (2005a) continues the study of the body as active and reactive through the study of time and the ontology of the body in time. Grosz argues that

> [t]he exploration of life – traditionally the purview of the biological sciences – is a fundamental feminist political concern, not because feminists must continue their ongoing suspicion regarding various forms of (male-dominated) biological research, but because feminists, and all theorists interested in the relations between subjectivity, politics, and culture, need to have a more nuanced, intricate account of the body's immersion and participation in the world if they are to develop political strategies to transform the existing social regulation of bodies, that is to change existing forms of biopower, of domination and exploitation. (2)

Among Grosz's other books are *Architecture from the Outside: Essays on Virtual and Real Space* (2001) and *Time Travels: Feminism, Nature, Power* (2005b).

Gynocentric: gynocentric means literally to view the world from a female perspective. Gynocentric views were developed to offset the **androcentric** views so pervasively held in philosophy and the natural and social sciences as well as other disciplines. Gynocentric models have forced the rethinking of several different theories and theoretical approaches. For example, in anthropology feminist anthropologists presented a gynocentric alternative to the man-the-hunter model of human evolution. The man-the-hunter model argues that hunting forced humans to evolve to have larger brains, function cooperatively, to develop tool use, etc. The gynocentric woman-the-gather model utilises much of the same evidence and artefacts to argue that the gathering of women is what moved evolution in its present direction. Gynocentric models and worldviews frequently require a revaluation of already existing data and evidence, finding new evidence and developing methodologies that call into question some of the core practices of a discipline. In more recent philosophy the term 'gynocentric' has become less popular. In its place feminist critique or feminist analysis are more frequently used.

See **background assumptions; Eurocentric; masculinist; objectivity**

H

Haraway, Donna: white US feminist biologist working in feminist science studies. Haraway employs **postmodern feminism** to provide a critique of scientific practice. She is the author of numerous books in **feminist science studies,** among them *Primate Visions* (1989), *Modest Witness at Second Millennium* (1997) and *Simians, Cyborgs and Women* (1991). Her 1991 book contains her most well-known and influential essay, 'Situated Knowledges: The Science Question in Feminism and the Privilege of Partial Perspective'. In this essay Haraway critiques the claims of **objectivity** by mainstream science studies and scientific practice. She argues that this type of objectivity is **disembodied** and attempts of provide a God's eye view that appropriates and destroys nature. She asserts that an **embodied, situated knowledge** will provide greater objectivity in the sciences. Situated knowledge is knowledge that is generated from local, particular, gendered, raced, classed contexts that result in a particular vision or perspective. All perspectives are partial and objectivity is the result of multiple, partial perspectives. In her later work, *Modest Witness at Second Millennium* Haraway furthers this argument with a methodology she calls **diffraction** which is a new critical consciousness that is a technology in itself and is an active, critical practice that subjects the ways we generate knowledge to analysis and change.

Harding, Sandra: white US feminist philosopher specialising in epistemology and feminist science studies. Sandra Harding provides one of the earliest critiques of the political and epistemological structure of science with her book *The Science Question in Feminism*(1986). She continued this contribution with her book *Whose Science? Whose Knowledge?* (1991), as the editor of *The 'Racial' Economy of Science: Toward a Democratic Future* (1993) and in *Is Science Multicultural?* (1998). Harding argues that scientific communities are designed, intentionally or not, to allow only a select, homogenous few in to scientific practice. Because members of the scientific community have a similar social location it is difficult, if not impossible, for them to recognise, or even desire to recognise, those historically, culturally and socially embedded practices and views that shape, inform and guide their processes of discovery and justification. Lack of democracy in science results in an epistemic **monoculture**, that is a homogeneity of knowledge that appears to be objective and value-neutral but is value-laden and is the result of 'weak objectivity.' Harding argues that the problem 'is not that individuals in the community are androcentric,

Eurocentric or economically overprivileged (though that certainly doesn't help)' (1992: 579), but that within this dominant discourse certain methodologies and modes of research have been made to appear to be normal/natural and unassailable. Harding argues for structural, methodological and ideological changes in science to increase the level of democracy and **objectivity** in science and to recognise that all knowledge is the result of **local knowledge** systems. This change is best achieved through a **standpoint epistemology**, an epistemology that initiates its questions from the perspective of marginal lives. Harding argues that the result of feminist standpoint epistemology is the possibility for **strong objectivity** and **strong/strategic reflexivity** that in turn are practices that can lead to greater epistemic pluralism and a more multicultural science.

See **feminist epistemology; feminist science studies**

Hartsock, Nancy: white US feminist philosopher specialising in epistemology. Nancy Hartsock, one of the earliest proponents of **standpoint epistemology**, is the author of *The Feminist Standpoint Revisited and Other Essays* (1999), *Money, Sex and Power: Toward a Feminist Historical Materialism* (1985). In *Feminist Standpoint Revisited* Hartsock continues her commitment to the connections between theory and practice and a willingness to work systematically through her own arguments. Hartsock states, '[i]n revisiting the argument I made for a feminist standpoint, I want to pluralize the idea and preserve its utility as an instrument of struggle against dominant groups' (239). Hartsock builds upon the insight of feminist standpoint theory, that the oppressed have a different, more critical view of reality than the dominant group, and moves away from a single, most critical view, that of a category 'women', to a standpoint that points to the knowledge generated from multiple, embodied, situated subjectivities. Hartsock's work on feminist standpoint theory has been important for a number of other feminist thinkers in their formulations of standpoint theory. For example, both **Sandra Harding** and **Patricia Hill Collins** are aided by Hartsock's work.

See **embodied; feminist epistemology; objectivity; oppression**

Hegemony/hegemonic: hegemony is the result of social institutions, practices and values of mainstream and dominant culture that covertly move all of culture along the dominant trajectory. Hegemonic norms construct a narrative around other practices and values to make them appear to be deviant, dangerous or unnatural. For example, heterosexuality is hegemonic in western culture. Lesbian, gay, bisexual or transgendered people are made to appear to be deviant and dangerous. Social institutions still make it legal to discriminate against gays and lesbians. Social practices continue to allow joking and harassment at the expense of LGBT people. Social values make gay bashing a sport, and social norms eroticise lesbian sexuality for the benefit of straight men.

Held, Virginia: white US feminist philosopher specialising in social and political philosophy, ethics of care and economics. Held is well-known for her work in **ethics of care,** an approach to ethics that values connectedness and the primacy of caring relationships, over the abstract principles that are the foundation for an ethics of justice. It is a view in which 'relationships between persons, rather than individual rights or individual preferences, are a primary focus' (Held, 2002: 31). In her book *The Ethics of*

Care: Personal, Political, and Global (2005) Held connects issues of justice to ethics of care arguing that care and justice are not mutually exclusive, but intertwined. She argues in 'Care and the Extension of Markets' (2002) that we can more accurately see what the limits and boundaries of the market should be through an ethics of care. Held claims that the commodification of the market value of caring activities – such as teaching, medicine, childcare – is one of the least appropriate ways in which to think of its value' (22). Caring work has its own intrinsic value free of its value in the marketplace and that

> [w]e should, then, recognize the enormous value of caring work – in expressing social connectedness, in contributing to children's development, and family satisfaction, and in enabling social cohesion and well being (the list could go on and on). And we should demand of society that such work, in all its various forms, be compensated in ways more in line than at present with its evaluated worth. . . . (21–2)

Held is also the author of *Rights and Goods: Justifying Social Action* (1989), *Feminist Morality: Transforming Culture, Society, and Politics* (1993).

Heteronormativity: the assumption that heterosexual behaviour is the norm biologically and socially. Assuming that a person's life partner is of the opposite sex is an example of heteronormativity, as is assuming that what counts as sex is penile-vaginal penetration and that gay men and lesbians can't have real sex. Furthermore, because our cultural is heteronormative many people probably deny or don't acknowledge sexual desires that are outside of the heteronormative mainstream. Thus it may be the case that in a less heteronormative society there would be more LGBT people. Many feminists have critiqued heternormativity. For example, **Luce Irigaray** provides a critique of heteronormativity in 'The Sex Which Is Not One' (1985a) as does **Judith Butler** in *Gender Trouble* (1990). **Marilyn Frye** critiques heteronormativity in 'To Be and To Be Seen' as well as other essays in her *Politics of Reality* (1983).

See **heterosexism**

Heterosexism: Audre Lorde in her essay 'I Am Your Sister: Black Women Organizing Across Sexualities' (1990) describes heterosexism as 'a belief in the inherent superiority of one form of loving over all others and therefore the right to dominance' (321). In her book *Lesbian Ethics* (1989) **Sarah Hoagland,** using the term 'heterosexualism', connects it directly to patriarchy and the oppression of women, while linking it to the need for a **lesbian ethics.** She states:

> Heterosexualism is men dominating and de-skilling women in any number of forms; from outright attack to paternalistic care, and women devaluing (of necessity) female bonding as well as finding inherent conflicts between commitment and autonomy, and consequently valuing an ethics of dependence. Heterosexualism is a way of living (which actual practitioners exhibit to a greater or lesser degree) that normalizes the dominance of one person in a relationship and the subordination of another. As a result it undermines female agency. (29)

Broadly understood, heterosexism is the structural **oppression** of LGBT (lesbian, gay, bisexual and transgendered) people and the normalising and naturalising of heterosexual relations and relations predicated on dominance. It exists in daily practices, laws, social practices and social structures. Daily practices such as assuming that a person's partner is of a different sex and that a male partner is the 'breadwinner' in a relationship are examples of heterosexism. Laws, such as banning same-sex marriages and sodomy laws, bans on gay and lesbians in the military and lax domestic violence laws, are examples of overt heterosexist laws. Social practices such as assuming that rape and domestic violence do not exist among LGBT couples and not showing intimate same-sex relations on mainstream television are examples of heterosexism that are equally as insidious as legal heterosexist measures. Furthermore, the refusal to construct laws to protect LGBT people and straight women from hate crimes, housing and employment discrimination, and the denial of coverage for partners by insurance companies are types of heterosexism that make a safe daily life impossible for many LGBT people.

See **heteronormativity**

Hoagland, Sarah: white, US feminist philosopher specialising in ethics and lesbian theory. Hoagland is the author of *Lesbian Ethics: Toward New Value* (1989). She argues that the category of lesbian, unlike the category 'women', is not intertwined with 'dominance and violence as norms of behavior' that are part of the **androcentric, Eurocentric** value system (Hoagland, 1994: 461). Because lesbians are outside of the dominant framework, they have the potential to choose a set of values that is meaningful to them and withdraw 'from the heterosexual value system' (1994: 461). Hoagland describes this as a type of metaphysical lesbian separatism, one that entails an ideological separatism instead of a physical separatism.

See **heteronormativity; lesbian ethics; separatism**

hooks, bell: African-American feminist literary theorist specialising in race and class theory and media analysis. Bell hooks is a pseudonym for Gloria Watkins. Hooks is an influential feminist literary theorist and a prolific writer. The first of her over thirty books was published in 1981. *Ain't I a Woman? Black Women and Feminism* (1981) examines the effects of slavery on Black womanhood and the resulting devaluation of Black women that has resulted in them having the lowest social status of any group in US culture. She also provides a critique of white feminism and Black liberation struggles arguing that they both alienate and devalue Black women. The feminist movement failed to take into account race and class and the differing needs of Black women. The Black liberation movement required that Black women put their race before their gender viewing feminist Black women as a threat to Black liberation. In her subsequent books hooks continues her critical analysis of the complexity of race, class and gender intersecting with popular culture, aesthetics, spirituality and relationships. Her 2000 book *Feminism Is for Everybody: Passionate Politics* (2000) provides an overview of major themes and issues in feminist theory. In this text hooks provides a definition of feminism, a definition that she initially developed in her 1984 book *Feminist Theory: From Margin to Center*, hooks states that feminism 'is a movement to end sexism, sexist exploitation and oppression' (1). She claims she likes this definition because it doesn't point to men as the problem, but points to patriarchy as the problem (1). Among hooks' other books are *Teaching to Transgress* (1994), *All About Love: New Visions* (2001), *The Will to Change: Men, Masculinity, and Love* (2004) and *Black Looks: Race and Representation* (1992).

See **Black feminist thought**

I

Imaginary: a concept used in postmodern feminism but developed by psychoanalyst Jacques Lacan (1981) to refer to a prelinguistic, narcissistic, mirroring stage in human development in which the concept of self and **other** are developed, with the other always understood in terms of the narcissistic self. **Judith Butler** writes '[t]he imaginary relation, the one constituted through narcissistic identification, is always tenuous precisely because it is an external object that is determined to be oneself' (1993: 152). Lacan argued that women never move beyond the imaginary phase because they never fully enter the **symbolic** realm of language and self. **Postmodern feminist** philosophy has utilised and critiqued Lacan's formulation of the imaginary. For example, **Luce Irigaray** develops a radical female imaginary in *This Sex Which Is Not One* (1985a) and *The Speculum of the Other Woman* (1985b). She writes in *This Sex Which Is Not One* that

> the rejection, the exclusion of a female imaginary certainly puts woman in the position of experiencing herself only fragmentarily, in the little-structured margins of a dominant ideology, as waste, or excess, what is left of a mirror invested by the (masculine) 'subject' to reflect himself. But if the female imaginary were to deploy itself, if it could bring itself into play otherwise than scraps, uncollected debris, would it represent itself, even so, in the form of one universe? (30)

Further reading: Lacan (1981)

Imperialism: the domination of one culture and/or country by another such that the values and practices of the dominating culture are forced to be absorbed by the dominated country. Sometimes this is done through the occupation of one country by another. For example, some argue that the US has imperialised Iraq not only through war, but also by requiring them to adhere to western democracy. Other examples of imperialism that some cite are the requirements by the International Monetary Fund of Third World countries to adhere to certain trade practices and guidelines in order to receive loans. Imperialism can also happen within a country between differing cultural narratives. For example, Black feminist thinkers such as **bell hooks** (1992) and **Patricia Hill Collins** (1991) have theorised how white culture imperialises Black culture through keeping African-Americans in low paying jobs and thus exploiting Black labour, normalising white experience and values. Thus occupation exists structurally, ideologically and physically.

Further reading: Mohanty (2003); Spivak (1988)

Intersex/Disorder of Sexual Development (DSD): the Intersex Society of North America (ISNA) characterises intersex/ DSD as a term used to describe a set of physical conditions 'in which a person is born with reproductive or sexual anatomy that doesn't seem to fit the typical definitions of female or male' (www.isna.org). Some of these conditions are diagnosed at birth, others later in life. Because people with intersex conditions challenge social norms regarding sex and gender, the physical conditions of intersex are frequently managed medically through surgery and hormonal treatment as well as socially through behavioural training. Thus the medical community and some parents work at reinforcing not just behavioural gender norms but the expectations of genital difference through surgery so that the essential congruity between sex and gender and the expectations of sexual dimorphism are replicated.

Anne Fausto-Sterling in *Sexing the Body* (2000) describes the history of the treatment of people with intersexed conditions as a 'most literal tale of social construction – the story of the emergence of strict surgical enforcement of a two-party system of sex...' (32). She argues that intersex conditions necessarily challenge the notion that **sex** is fixed and biological and **gender** is purely a social construct and seeks a more dynamic view of sex and gender, one that will not be so destructive of the lives of those with intersexed conditions.

Recently intersex activists have come to prefer the term Disorder of Sexual Development because it allows them to work more fruitfully with the medical community. According to Sherri Groveman Morris in 'DSD But Intersex Too: Shifting Paradigms Without Abandoning Roots' (2006) '[p]rior to the adoption of "DSD" as the preferred term, there was apparently some confusion about whether certain medical conditions properly fell under the heading of "intersex." ISNA's avowed aim in preferring "DSD" is to support improved medical care for children born with such conditions' (1).

See **Butler, Judith; essentialism; social construction**
Further reading: Butler (2004)

Irigaray, Luce: French postmodern feminist psychoanalyst. Irigaray is one of the foremost figures in **postmodern feminism**. Her texts, *The Speculum of the Other Woman* (1985b) and *This Sex Which is Not One* (1985a), articulate the ways women and the feminine have been left out of **androcentric** discourse. Working from the psychoanalytic tradition, Irigaray approaches her argument through an analysis of the continuity of language and sexuality. She argues that the **phallocentrism** of language and the western philosophical tradition fail to represent women's desires, suppress the feminine and mistakenly model female sexuality through male sexuality. She argues 'that the *feminine occurs only within models and laws devised by male subjects*' (1985a: 86) and that 'often prematurely emitted, makes him miss . . . what her own pleasure might be all about' (1985a: 91). Thus rejected,

> the exclusion of a female imaginary certainly puts woman in the position of experiencing herself only fragmentarily, in the little-structured margins of a dominant ideology, as waste, or excess, what is left of a mirror invested by the (masculine) 'subject' to reflect himself. But if the female imaginary were to deploy itself, if it could bring itself into play otherwise than scraps, uncollected debris, would it represent itself, even so, in the form of one universe? (1985a: 30)

Irigaray argues that women can create their own feminine sexuality, one that is plural, modelled on their own sexual organs, the labia that are already two and maybe more, and their own orgasms as multiple. She states '[h]er sexuality is at least double, goes even further; it is plural' (1985a: 32). Just as the **phallocentric** order translates from sexuality through to language and theory, so does female sexuality. Feminine theory, language and social order will thus be multiple and pluralistic.

Iterability: a term used by French deconstructionist Jacques Derrida to point to the necessary repeatability of language. Derrida argues repetition is what already structures language and makes it have meaning and accessibility.

Postmodern feminist and **queer theorist Judith Butler** argues in *Bodies That Matter* (1994) that **performativity** must be understood through the process of iterability, which she describes as a 'regularized and constrained repetition of norms' or ritualised repetition (95). Butler argues that performativity is not a repetition

> performed *by* a subject; this repetition is what enables a subject and constitutes the temporal condition of the subject. This iterability implies that 'performance' is not a singular 'act' or event, but a ritualised production, a ritual reiterated under and through constraint, under and through the force of prohibition and taboo, with the threat of ostracism and even death controlling and compelling the shape of the production, but not, I will insist, determining it fully in advance. (95)

Through this 'logic of iterability' sexuality and gender are directed along **hegemonic** cultural norms.

J

Jaggar, Alison: white US feminist philosopher specialising in social and political philosophy. Alison Jaggar is a **socialist feminist** and one of the founding members of the **Society for Women in Philosophy**. Her book *Feminist Politics and Human Nature* (1988) provides a sweeping critique of the branches of feminist social and political philosophy. Jaggar analyses **liberal feminism, Marxist feminism, radical feminism** and **socialist feminism** by sifting through their underlying views of human nature and assessing their viability for a politically effective feminist theory. Jaggar argues in favour of socialist feminism, showing the epistemological and ethical viability of socialist feminism and the **standpoint epistemology** that comes out of it.

K

Kittay, Eva: white US feminist philosopher specialising in ethics, social and political philosophy, and disability studies. Kittay is the author of *Love's Labor: Essays on Women, Equality, and Dependency* (1999) in which she provides an analysis of the **androcentric** myth of independence and how it generates a false view of gender and race equality. She develops what she calls a 'dependency critique'. The dependency critique 'is a feminist critique of equality that asserts: A conception of society viewed as an association of equals masks inequitable dependencies, those of infancy and childhood, old age, illness and disability' (xi). Kittay argues that in order to believe the fiction of independence, we must ignore parts of our collective lives and continue to exclude 'large portions of the population from the domain of equality' (xiii). She puts forth a notion of equality that she calls 'connection-based equality' that is based on the basic human need for relationships and what types of obligations people have based on the connections they have. Kittay is also the author of *Metaphor: Its Cognitive Force and Linguistic Structure* (1987) and co-editor of *Theoretical Perspectives on Dependency and Women* (2002).

See **ethics of care**

Kristeva, Julia: Bulgarian-French postmodern psychoanalyst. Kristeva's work brings to feminist philosophy the distinction between the **semiotic** and the **symbolic**, the notion of the **abject**, and an increased attention to the body. Kristeva defines the semiotic as one of two elements of language. The semiotic is the rhythm, tones and organisation of language through which 'bodily drives are *discharged*' and are 'meaningful parts of language and yet do not represent or signify something' (Kristeva and Oliver, 1997: xiv). It is the part of language that is non-linguistic and is the result of the bodily need to communicate. Symbolic denotes 'the structure or grammar that governs the ways in which symbols can refer . . . and is the domain of position and judgment' (Kristeva and Oliver, 1997: xv). The semiotic gives symbols meaning, thus language begins work at the level of the body. Kristeva develops the term abject in her book *The Power of Horror* to indicate the visceral horror humans experience when confronted by those aspects of themselves and life that force them to confront their own materiality. The abject is the experience of the fear and revulsion of one's own impurity and materiality. All bodily functions are abject, especially those associated with waste or decay. Kristeva states '[i]t is not lack of cleanliness or health that causes abjection but what disturbs identity, the system, order' (4). The corpse and the maternal body are used by Kristeva as primary examples of the abject. One's confrontation with a corpse, especially of a person to whom one is close, forces one not just to confront one's own death symbolically, but to experience and confront the horror of the possibility of one's death. In Kristeva's words: 'The corpse (or cadaver: cadere, to fall), that which has irremediably come a cropper, is cesspool, and death; it upsets even more violently the one who confronts it as fragile and fallacious chance' (3). The maternal body represents expulsion, fruitfulness and generative power that is repulsive and threatening to the **phallocentric** order. Abject is an especially useful concept for feminists because Kristeva argues that all female bodies are viewed as inherently abject by **patriarchal** culture. Kristeva uses the concept to help explain repression and **oppression**.

See **postmodern feminism**

Further reading: Kristeva and Oliver (1997)

Latina feminism: see **Chicana feminism and Latina feminism**

Le Dœuff, Michèle: white French feminist philosopher specialising in epistemology and history of ideas. Le Dœuff is among a small group of female philosophers in France who actively consider themselves to be feminist. In her essay 'Feminism Is Back in France – Or Is It?' (2000) Le Dœuff argues sex equality is selective and inconsistent in France and that one can only be heard if one's views are on the public agenda. Thus there is a sort of selective censorship of ideas, especially those related to feminist issues. Le Dœuff argues that

> [t]here is, rather, a careful selection of themes and a kind of discrete regulation. Yes to the project of having more women in Parliament and in government. Yes to introducing (in fact, reintroducing) the use of the female grammatical gender for professional women (*la minister, una avocate*). But no to our demands for important amendments to reproductive rights legislation, and particularly those amendments which would benefit immigrant women and teenagers, who still don't have normal access to these rights. Yes to some strategies to increase sex equality in education and to encourage more girls to do maths and sciences. But no to serious dissemination of information at school about contraception. (245)

In her book *The Sex of Knowing* (2003a) Le Dœuff engages in genealogy of knowing as gendered. She creates links between the legitimacy of male knowing and the institutionalisation and enculturation of women as not knowers and as 'cognitively paralyzed' such that women are 'incapable of recognising violence for what it was, even when she was experiencing it' (xv). She argues that the structure of the academy, public life and social policy perpetuate women's subordination. Le Dœuff is also the author of *The Philosophical Imaginary* (2003b).

Further reading: Deutscher (2001)

Lesbian Ethics: Sarah Hoagland argues in her original 1989 book *Lesbian Ethics: Toward New Value* that the category of lesbian, unlike the category 'women', is not intertwined with 'dominance and subordination as norms of behavior. And . . . that by attending each other, we may find the possibility of ethical values appropriate to lesbian existence, values we can choose as moral agents to give meaning to our lives as lesbians' (see Hoagland, 1994: 461). With a lesbian ethic, lesbians have the potential to choose a value system outside of these norms that is meaningful to them and withdraw 'from the heterosexual value system' (1994: 461). Hoagland thus seeks to generate strategies to create meaning and value under systematic oppression. She desecribes this strategic withdrawal from the heterosexual value system as a type of metaphysical lesbian separatism – one that entails an ideological separatism instead of a physical separatism. It also entails a reassertion of female **agency** as independent and challenges the dependency model of female agency asserted by heterosexism.

Marilyn Frye, in her essay 'A Response to *Lesbian Ethics*: Why *Ethics*?' (1991), claims that 'ethics' is not what is needed by lesbians. She argues that 'ethics' is really a misnomer in Hoagland's title, *Lesbian Ethics*. Hoagland is not seeking 'ethics' in any traditional sense; that is she is not trying to develop a system that is preoccupied with the good and the right. These are too invested in patri-archy, whiteness and dominance. Frye states:

> It would behoove women who claim to abhor race and class privilege to give up the habit of pursuing them by being and trying to be good. The discov-ery that one is not good, or doesn't know how to be good, might be welcomed as releasing one from the game of good and evil and thus from the will-bindings that keep us bonded to our oppressors. (58)

Instead what a lesbian ethics seeks, and what Hoagland is articulating in her text, is learning what to 'pay atten-tion to' (58) and how to create meaning free from the heterosexist system. 'Such an "ethics" makes no pretense at all of telling us what is right or how to be good, but I think if it is allowed, it can seduce those of us who feel we need such things into a new space much further from our citizen-fathers' homes, where "right" and "good" no longer trick us into continuing our roles as dutiful daugh-ters' (59).

See **feminist ethics**

Liberal Feminism: liberal feminism has its roots in the eigh-teenth century with Mary Wollstonecraft, Harriet Taylor Mill and John Stuart Mill and is characterised by a persis-tent faith in reason and rationality. Contemporary liberal feminists tend to agree that the values (life, liberty and the pursuit of happiness) and structures of liberal democracy have the potential to allow for the end of the oppression of women if women were allowed to fully participate in these values and structures. Thus, unlike **radical feminists** and **socialist feminists**, liberal feminists do not believe that there needs to be new political, economic and social cat-egories to end gender oppression. Liberal feminists want women fully enfranchised into the social systems of corporate, government, economic and educational life and work to end gender segregation, gender discrimination in all areas of public life and gender-based laws. They seek legal and public solutions to the problems affecting women. With their roots in classical liberalism, feminist liberalism relies upon rationality and the 'reasoned argument' to create change (Jaggar, 1988: 181). Liberal feminists have advocated for such issues as accessible and adequate childcare, **reproductive rights**, job retraining, work places free of **sexual harassment** and equality in education. The National Organization for Women and Planned Parenthood are characterised as a liberal feminist organisation.

Further reading: Mill (2002); Taylor Mill (1998); Wollstonecraft (1988)

Lloyd, Genevieve: white Australian feminist philosopher specialising in history of modern philosophy and epistemology. Lloyd is the author of *The Man of Reason: 'Male' and 'Female' in Western Philosophy* (1984), an important contribution to the feminist study of the history of philosophy. Lloyd argues that the understanding of **reason** that is ensconced within philosophy and western culture is gendered masculine; that is, it is viewed as an attribute of males and not females. Lloyd traces this lineage back to Plato and through the Modern period to twentieth-century existentialism. Lloyd argues that with the rise of Modern philosophy and the dominance of the Cartesian methodological approach to acquiring reason, being a 'man of reason' became a virtuous quality, both epistemically and socially. Lloyd is also the co-author with **Moira Gatens** of *Collective Imaginings: Spinoza, Past and Present* (1999b) and the editor of *Feminism and the History of Philosophy* (2002).

Local Knowledge: many feminist epistemologists characterise all knowledge as local knowledge. In other words, they argue that all knowledge is generated by the conditions, beliefs and values of the culture from which it originates. Claims of truth, **objectivity** and universality are claims that hold within that particular knowledge system and may or may not hold outside of the system.

See **ecological thinking; feminist epistemology; situated knowledge; social construction; universal**

Further reading: Harding (1998); Longino (1990)

Longino, Helen: white, US feminist philosopher specialising in philosophy of science and epistemology. Longino's work in philosophy of science can be characterised as **feminist empiricism**. Her 1990 book *Science as Social Knowledge: Values and Objectivity in Scientific Inquiry* helped usher in several significant works in **feminist epistemology** and **feminist science studies** in the 1990s. In this text she argues that science should be understood to be a social practice. She further argues that this social nature of science goes to the very core of scientific practice not only through the context of discovery, those things that lead to the initial discovery of a theory or entity, but also to the context of justification, those practices that determine the viability of a theory or the existence of an entity. Because science is a social practice that is infused with the values and norms of the community that generates it, one might question whether an objective science is possible. Longino argues that scientific knowledge contains **background assumptions** as well as **contextual values,** which are non-cognitive values that are not strictly part of the practices of science but nonetheless play a role in scientific decision-making in addition to cognitive values. She asserts that **objectivity** in scientific practice is not a matter of all or nothing, but is a matter of the degree to which a community practices a set of criteria that Longino argues is objectivity promoting. Among these is equality of intellectual authority, community response and shared community standards. In her 2002 book *The Fate of Knowledge* Longino again studies the social nature of scientific practice arguing that those debates in philosophy of science that seek to focus on the rational nature of science or the social nature of science are failing to understand that what we call scientific knowledge or science's cognitive capacities are themselves social or interactive. Furthermore, Longino argues that scientific knowledge needs to be studied in its complex local contexts.

Lorde, Audre (1934–1992): African-American feminist poet, essayist and activist. Lorde's poetry and essays have been very influential in feminist philosophy. She is a co-founder of the Kitchen Table: Women of Color Press. She is continually intentional about her race, her lesbian sexual identity and her feminist perspective permeating all her work. Perhaps her most cited and most influential essay in philosophy is 'The Master's Tools Will Never Dismantle the Master's House' in *Sister Outsider* (1984). In this essay Lorde provides a two-pronged critique against **patriarchy** and mainstream white feminism. Lorde argues that feminists that think they can use the methods/tools of patriarchy in an attempt to subvert patriarchy are seriously mistaken because by using patriarchy's methods they are falling prey to patriarchy, replicating patriarchal practices, therefore furthering patriarchy and not achieving their feminist goals.

Another of her influential essays, 'Scratching the Surface: Some Notes on Barriers to Women and Loving' in *Sister Outsider* (1984), illustrates how the term lesbian was used as a way to keep women from forming collectively and working together. She states:

Today the red-herring of lesbian-baiting is being used in the Black community to obscure the true face of racism/sexism. Black women sharing close ties with each other, politically or emotionally, are not the enemies of Black men. Too frequently, however, some Black men attempt to rule by fear those Black women who are more ally than enemy. These tactics are expressed as threats of emotional rejection: 'Their poetry wasn't too bad but I couldn't take all those lezzies.' The Black man saying this is code-warning every Black woman present interested in a relationship with a man – and most Black women are – that (1) if she wishes to have her work considered by him she must eschew any other allegiance except to him and (2) any woman who wishes to retain his friendship and/or support had better not be 'tainted' by woman-identified interests. (45)

Lorde makes clear that not only the political risks Black women face when they want to unite, but their bodies and lives are at risk. Lorde argues that as long as the term 'lesbian' can be used as a derogatory term and threat against women, all women, straight and lesbian, are physically and politically at risk. Lorde died of cancer in 1992. She wrote about her experience with breast cancer and her mastectomy in her book *The Cancer Journals* (1980). Among her books are *Sister Outsider* (1984), which contains 'The Master's Tools Will Never Dismantle the Master's House' and 'Some Notes on Barriers to Women and Loving', *Zami: A New Spelling of My Name* (1983) and *The Black Unicorn* (1995).

See **Black feminist thought**

Lugones, María: Latina feminist philosopher from Argentina teaching in the US, specialising in ethics, social and political philosophy, race theory, Latin American philosophy.

Lugones is known for her theories of 'world'-traveling, liminality and complex communication. In her essay 'Playfulness, "World"-Traveling, and Loving Perception' (1987), Lugones describes "world" traveling, as a practice of the oppressed who wilfully shift 'from the mainstream construction of life where she is constructed as an outsider to the other construction of life where she is more or less "at home" ' (3). The ' "world"-traveler' recognises her own multiplicity and is able to 'read[...] reality as multiple' (2006: 79). The marginalised occupy a liminal space, a space that is at the borders of the mainstream in which they can transgress the dominant ideology (2006: 76). Liminality necessitates ' "world"-traveling', as well as a recognition of one's multiplicity, an awareness of how dominant culture has constructed oneself and a sense of the self-construction of one's self.

Recognising others on the limen and recognising that they have lived their lives against the grain is necessary for complex communication. Lugones argues:

> If I think that you are in a limen, I will know that some of the time, you do not mean what you say but something else. Sometimes, it is in the form of what you say that conveys most of the meaning, a form of sharp contrast with the dominant mainstream . . . So it is not true that if we stand together in the limen we will understand each other, we can make the weaker claim that if we recognize each other as occupying liminal sites, then we will have a disposition to read each other away from structural, dominant meaning, or have good reason to do so as oppressed peoples. (2006: 79)

Complex communication is opaque and cannot be reduced to the experiences of one's own experiential vocabulary. Thus it takes creativity and the creation of meaning (2006: 84). Lugones is also the author of *Pilgrimages/Peregrinajes: Theorizing Coalition Against Multiple Oppressions* (2003).

See **Chicana feminism and Latina feminism; marginalised; oppression**

M

Mahowald, Mary: white US feminist philosopher specialising in medical ethics. Mahowald is the author of *Women and Children in Health Care: An Unequal Majority* (1996) and *Genes, Women and Equity* (2000) as well as the editor one of the earliest academic feminist anthologies, *The Philosophy of Woman: Classical to Current Concepts* (1977). Mary Mahowald argues in *Genes, Women and Equity* that genetic interventions are not **gender, race** or **class** neutral. Women pay a disproportionate burden of the invasive technology that accompanies genetic technology. Furthermore, most genetic **reproductive technology** benefits white middle- and upper-class, educated women.

Marginalised: to be marginalised means to experience a variety of conditions that are oppressive. Feminists usually speak of groups who are marginalised and people who are marginalised as a result of being part of that group. Groups who are marginalised might not be allowed adequate political representation or a voice in decisions or actions that affect their lives. They are relegated to the margins in terms of being pushed or kept outside of mainstream social, epistemological and political life. Some feminists argue that one result of being marginalised is the ability to have a more critical view of society because those that are outside of the mainstream have less of an investment in maintaining the present social structure. They are more likely to offer alternative ethical, epistemological and political views than those that are benefited from the current social arrangements. The view from the position of the marginalised is called **standpoint epistemology**.

See **oppression**

Marxist Feminism: Friedrich Engels' *The Origin of the Family* (1884/1972), a fundamental text in Marxist feminism, argued that the move to private property included a shift from **matriarchy** to **patriarchy** and was the initiating point for women's subordination and **oppression**. Monogamy and patriarchy are products of the need for a secure transfer of wealth and property. Because gender oppression is a product of **class** oppression, overthrowing capitalism is the means for ending women's oppression. Due to the focus on class, most Marxist feminists focus on the problems women face in the workforce and class-based access to goods (Tong, 1998). For example, they point to the gender division of labour and women's underpayment for their work and they highlight the lack a payment for household work, the second-shift of childcare and household work that most women perform after they come home from their 'real' work, the **sexual division of labour**, the commodification of women's bodies for sexual, reproductive and entertainment purposes, and the classed nature of access to **reproductive technology** and healthcare technology. Marxist feminism has heavily influenced **socialist feminism** and this is where much of the Marxist-influenced work is now occurring.

Further reading: Jaggar (1988)

Masculinist: a theory, action, principle or value is masculinist when it presents a view that reflects only the experiences of men in a culture and thus presents an incomplete and inaccurate view of the social, epistemological, ethical and political arrangements of that culture. Masculinist theories or practices not only deny the experiences of women as important and worthy of study, they also deny the importance of women and women's voices in the generation of knowledge, ethical decision-making and political activity.

See **androcentric**

Matriarchy: matriarchy means 'mother rule'. It is used to describe communities or ideologies in which women, usually mothers, hold the most social and political power. Friedrich Engels in *The Origins of the Family* [1884] (1972) argued that matriarchy was a more primitive historical social state than **patriarchy** and the move to patriarchy signalled social progress. Many feminist historians have argued that true matriarchal communities have not existed historically; instead there have been matrilineal societies, societies where parental identification is passed through the mother, not the father. Some separatist feminists have thought critically about what it would mean to construct a matriarchal community. For example, the arguments of **Mary Daly** in *Gyn/Ecology* (1978) have influenced feminist philosophy on numerous levels. In *Gyn/Ecology* Daly envisions what it would be like if women experienced life in a matriarchal society instead of living under patriarchy.

See **separatism**

Mimétisme: see **strategic essentialism**

Misogyny: misogyny literally means the hatred of women. Feminists have shown that misogyny exists at numerous social levels as well as at individual levels. Individually we can point to men or women, though obviously we are more likely to point to men, as misogynists. For example, the nineteenth-century philosopher Friedrich Nietzsche has been cited by some feminists as a misogynist, a woman-hater, because of his apparent disdain of women and the feminine. Social institutions can be misogynistic through the laws, policies and practices they put forth. For example, one could argue that the welfare reform of the 1990s was not only racist, but also misogynist in that the reform specifically targeted, affected and harmed poor women.

Mitchell, Juliet: white British psychoanalyst specialising in gender theory and sibling relations. In 1974 Juliet Mitchell published *Psychoanalysis and Feminism*, the first sustained study of the usefulness of psychoanalysis for feminism. Mitchell wrote this text during the height of **second wave feminism** in which psychoanalysis was argued to be a patriarchal structure that contributed to the oppression of women. Mitchell, on the contrary, argues that psychoanalysis is necessary for understanding women's oppression. She asserts that part of the task of psychoanalysis has been to provide an analysis of patriarchal culture and that it is does not merely serve as a tool of patriarchy. Mitchell analyses the work of feminists **Simone de Beauvoir**, Kate Millet, **Shulamith Firestone** and Betty Friedan arguing that they deny the existence of the unconscious in favour of socialisation as an explanation for female oppression. Because of this they cannot theoretically explain the internalisation of sexual difference and the universality of women's oppression.

Mitchell's *Madmen and Medusa: Reclaiming Hysteria* (2001) and *Siblings: Sex and Violence* (2003) study sibling relationships, hysteria and violence. She points out that psychoanalysis has focused on vertical familial relationships, in other words child–parent relationships, and has neglected horizontal relationships, in other words sibling relationships. These horizontal, or what she calls 'lateral', relations are essential for understanding the construction of sex differences, as well as for understanding learned, internalised behaviours of violence and domination. In *Madmen and Medusa* Mitchell considers hysteria as a **universal** condition, thus a condition of both men and women as well as of all cultures. She argues that this is an important insight for feminism because it can explain the cross-cultural oppression of women, as well as male violence and the expression and repression of male anger. Mitchell is also the author of *Women, the Longest Revolution: Essays on Feminism, Literature, and Psychoanalysis* (1984) and *Women's Estate* (1972).

Mohanty, Chandra Talpade: Indian feminist theorist teaching in the US, specialising in postcolonial feminist theory and Third World feminism. Mohanty is an important figure in **Third World feminism** and **postcolonial theory**. Her essay 'Under Western Eyes: Feminist Scholarship and Colonial Discourses' in Mohanty et al. (1991) represents a significant early text in feminist postcolonial theory through its critique of western feminism. In this essay she critiques western feminism for making a monolith of Third World women. In effect western feminism has colonised the lives, experiences and writings of Third World women by constructing what Mohanty calls the 'third world difference', a static category that seeks to explain how all Third World women are oppressed. Mohanty argues that her position is not against generalisations per se, but that it is for 'careful, historically specific generalizations responsive to complex strategies' (69).

Her 2003 collection of essays, *Feminism Without Borders: Decolonizing Theory, Practicing Solidarity*, puts forth an **anti-capitalist, anti-racist, transnational feminism,** arguing that feminism and capitalism are incompatible if feminism has as a goal cultural, economic and political transformation. This analysis will entail 'a critique of the operation, discourse, and values of capitalism and of their naturalization through neoliberal ideology and corporate culture' (9). Mohanty argues for a sustained critique of and activism against globalisation and corporatisation. Furthermore, in this text she 'revisits' her 1991 essay 'Under Western Eyes'. She works to consider the place of this essay in the twenty-first century and argues that 'Under Western Eyes' in the twenty-first century must take into consideration native or indigenous struggles and how these affect coalition building in Third World feminism. Mohanty is a co-editor of *Third World Women and the Politics of Feminism* (1991) and *Feminist Genealogies, Colonial Legacies, Democratic Futures* (1996).

See **colonialism**

Monoculture: feminist ecologist Vandana Shiva uses the term 'monoculture' to denote a lack of diversity that exists in multiple and intertwined ways. First, monoculture refers to a lack of agricultural and ecological diversity. For example, she argues in *Biopiracy* (1997) that genetic reductionism, seed sterilisation and large-scale corporate control of agriculture leads to agricultural monocultures. Second, monocultures refer to the lack of diversity of values, ideas and knowledge. In *Monocultures of the Mind* (1993) Shiva argues that western value systems and practices are creating a world monoculture by pirating the knowledge of indigenous communities, by requiring those cultures to adopt western values and practice to receive aid and by deligitimating the knowledge of other cultures as folk knowledge and 'common knowledge' and not the product of generations of community knowing.

See **colonialism; local knowledge; oppression**

$\boxed{\text{N}}$

Narayan, Uma: Indian feminist philosopher teaching in the US, specialising in ethics and social and political philosophy.) In her 1997 book *Dislocating Cultures: Identities, Traditions, and Third-World Feminism* Narayan analyses how the discourse of **colonialism** still distorts First World feminist and Third World fundamentalist understandings of **Third World feminism**. Narayan begins by providing an intentionally narrow description of Third World feminists as 'feminists who acquired feminist views and engaged in feminist politics in Third World countries' (4). She does this as part of her methodology of addressing the larger issue she seeks to address, the distorted understandings of Third World feminism by both the First and the Third World. Narayan uses this narrow definition as a way of arguing against the fundamentalist Third World view that feminism is a western product. If there are Third World women who arrive at feminist consciousness via their own experiences, then feminism cannot be a western import. Furthermore, Narayan seeks to argue against the idea that concerns expressed by Third World feminists are mere duplications of concerns expressed by western feminists. Narayan also analyses colonial discourse in the works of feminist writers, giving particular attention to **Mary Daly's** essay on *sati* in *Gyn/Ecology* (1978). Narayan expresses as primary concerns the continual need to locate issues within their national context and the need for critical and careful use of 'culture' and 'tradition' as modes of explanation. Narayan is also the co-editor of *Decentering the Center: Philosophy for a Multicultural, Postcolonial, and Feminist World* (2002), *Having and Raising Children: Unconventional Families, Hard Choices, and the Social Good* (1999) and *Reconstructing Political Theory: Feminist Perspectives* (1997).

See **decolonisation; transnational feminism**

Nelson, Lynn Hankinson: white US feminist philosopher specialising in philosophy of science and science studies. **Feminist empiricist** Lynn Hankinson Nelson develops an account of evidence based on the theories of the philosopher W. V. O. Quine in her book *Who Knows? From Quine to a Feminist Empiricism* (1989). Nelson argues that contrary to mainstream epistemology and philosophy of science, the appropriate epistemic **agent** is not the individual but the community. Furthermore, she argues that our experiences of **gender** should enter into our considerations of theories and evidence.

See **feminist epistemology; feminist science studies**

Noddings, Nel: white US feminist philosopher specialising in the ethics of care and philosophy of education. Noddings' work in feminist philosophy crosses over into her work on philosophy of education which is targeted at educators. In her book *Caring: A Feminine Approach to Ethics and Moral Education* (2nd edn, 2003), Noddings argues for an **ethics of care** generated from what she calls 'natural caring'. Natural caring is like the relationship mothers have with infants. When an infant needs care, mothers 'do not begin by formulating or solving a problem but by sharing a feeling. . . . [they] receive it and [they] react to it' (31). Noddings argues that this type of care is accessible to all humans and is universal, but it does not consist of universal moral judgements. She utilises natural caring as a way of understanding what our moral relationships should be like such as with education, each other, animals and plants. Among Noddings' other books are *Critical Lessons: What Our Schools Should Teach* (2006a), *Starting at Home: Caring and Social Policy* (2006b) and *Happiness and Education* (2004).

Nussbaum, Martha C.: white US feminist philosopher specialising in social and political philosophy, ethics and ancient philosophy. Nussbaum is a **liberal feminist** who is a prolific writer and has made many contributions to feminist philosophy. One particular such contribution is her work in the area of **gender** and development. Nussbaum develops the capabilities approach of Amartya Sen and applies it to the lives of women in developing countries. In her book *Women and Human Development: The Capabilities Approach* (2001) Nussbaum argues that it is the job of liberal democracy to provide its citizens with opportunities to realise their capabilities – what people are capable of doing or becoming – such that all people's needs are met at the minimum threshold required for the development of the whole community. Nussbaum formulates a capabilities approach that is attentive to different needs and capacities while at the same time universalist; it is compatible with distributive justice and generated from a Marxist-Aristotelian framework. Nussbaum applies her capabilities approach to the situation of poor and marginally poor women in India, though she argues that it is applicable to the situation of all women. Among Nussbaum's other books are *Sex and Social Justice* (2000), *Love's Knowledge: Essays on Philosophy and Literature* (1992) and *Hiding from Humanity: Disgust, Shame, and the Law* (2004).

See **universal**

O

Objectify: to objectify a woman is to see her as an object not as a subject with her own ends. It is a type of **gender oppression**. Feminists have argued that women are objectified in various ways. For example, some feminists argue that women are objectified when they are treated only as sexual objects for another's pleasure, such as through pornography; when they are **essentialised** as embodying and primarily consisting of certain traits, such as nurturing; when they are subject to **sexual harassment**; when legal measures take control away from their choices, for example the recent measures in the US that threaten to overturn *Roe* v. *Wade* that legalised women's right to safe legal abortion. **Classism, racism** and **heteronormative** discrimination lead to the objectification of people of colour and gay men and lesbians.

Objectivity: there are at least three interrelated ways to think of objectivity: as a practice, as a property and as a state of being. Objectivity as a practice means that it is a method or practice of arriving at a conclusion. One engages in objective practices, such as applying scientific methodology or distancing oneself from one's subject. This type of engagement is thought to lead to 'better' knowledge. 'Better' knowledge is the next sense in which one can understand objectivity. Knowledge arrived at through objective practices is objective knowledge – value-free, neutral, true knowledge. The third sense of understanding objectivity is that people are objective. They are able to practise (the first sense) objectivity and are thus themselves objective. The perception is that these people are able to arrive at more objective knowledge (the second sense of objectivity).

Feminists have provided critiques of objectivity in most areas of philosophy. For example, in the philosophy of science **Sandra Harding** has described the above types of objectivity as 'weak' objectivity, objectivity that prioritises neutral, value-free practice and knower. She has argued for **strong objectivity**, which requires that scientists recognise themselves as historically, culturally and socially located subjects and knowledge gathering that includes values that help to create strong objectivity such as 'fairness, honesty and detachment, which are moral and, indeed, [some] political values and interests' (1992: 579). **Postmodern feminist Susan Bordo** in *The Flight to Objectivity* (1987) argues that the history of western philosophy has centred on the Cartesian desire for a value-neutral location from which to view reality.

See **rationality; social construction; strategic/strong reflexivity**

Okin, Susan Moller (1946–2004): white New Zealand-born US feminist specialising in social and political philosophy. Okin's *Women in Western Political Thought* (1979) was one of the first texts that argued for the study of women as central to social and political philosophy. In *Justice, Gender and the Family* (1989) Okin extends this view to the family as an economic unit using a revised version of Rawls's distributive justice to argue that family life is structured by **gender** and is largely unjust. In her last and in some ways most well-known and controversial work *Is Multi-Culturalism Bad for Women?* (1999), Okin points to a tension between feminism and multiculturalism due to multiculturalism's commitment to the right to preserve cultural integrity. Okin argues that commitments to rights for minority cultures have a greater impact on women and girls and allow minority cultures to perpetuate violent and **misogynist** practices such as female genital mutilation, forced marriage to one's rapist, childhood marriage, polygamy and veiling.

Oppression: oppression is a multi-faceted experience that consists of having an outside force limit, arrange or constrain (sometimes physically and violently) an individual's or collective's life or aspects of their life. People are oppressed based on their race, gender, class, sexuality and ability. Oppression entered feminist theory as a conceptual category through **Marxist feminism** (Jaggar, 1988) and has been used to think about many aspects of women's experience and feminism, including how to define feminism. For example, **bell hooks** defines feminism through the work to end oppression. She states '[f]eminism is the movement to end sexism, sexist exploitation, and oppression' (2000: viii). In her essay 'Oppression' *The Politics of Reality* (1983) **Marilyn Frye** starts off by describing oppression as to 'Mold. Immobilize. Reduce' (2). Frye uses her now well-known analogy of the birdcage to further describe the experience of oppression. Frye argues that if you look at each individual wire of a birdcage you cannot see why the bird doesn't just fly around it, but if you look at the whole cage it is 'perfectly obvious that the bird is surrounded by a network of systematically related barriers, no one of which would be the least hindrance to its flight, but which, by their relations to each other, are as confining as the solid walls of a dungeon' (5). Like the birdcage, oppression is a system of interconnected barriers whose power can only be understood by seeing the connections and how they function together to diminish, impede, weaken, marginalise and confine one's daily life.

Feminists have analysed the effects of women's oppression on multiple levels such as reproduction, employment, self-determination, domestic violence, political voice, body image, pornography and sexuality, working to make clear how these are all part of a larger system of oppression. Feminists of colour, such as **Patricia Hill Collins, Chandra Talpade Mohanty, Gayatri Spivak, bell hooks** and **Gloria Anzaldúa** have argued that while white, western feminism has actively worked to end women's oppression it has oppressed women of colour. Collins argues that white feminist scholarship spoke authoritatively about Black women's experiences while at the same time dismissing Black women's ideas (1991). Spivak argues that the **subaltern** woman is further oppressed by those in postcolonial studies when they assume that her voice is self-evident and they attempt to speak for her (Spivak, 1988).

Other/Othering: a term first used in existential philosophy by Jean Paul Sartre to indicate the negative relation between individuals in which one has selfhood and views another as 'other', different and not-self. **Simone de Beauvoir** in *The Second Sex* (1952) expands upon Sartre's notion of the Other by developing this concept to explain social relations and women's subordination (Simons, 2000). Beauvoir sets out to address 'Why woman is the Other' (33). She argues that in all situations, perspectives and experiences woman is Othered because man sets himself as the norm and with selfhood while women is constructed as deviant and Other and exists only in relation to man, thus without selfhood.

The concept of the Other has expanded to many other areas of feminist philosophy, most notably **postmodern feminism** and **Third World feminism**. For example, postmodernist **Hélène Cixous** in 'Sorties' argues that the othering of women is essential to keeping the **phallocentric** social order running. But if women use their otherness against this system it would destabilise it. She writes:

> The challenging of this solidarity of logocentricism and phallocentricism has today become insistent enough – the bringing to light the fate which has been imposed upon women, of her burial – to threaten the stability of the masculine edifice which passed itself off as eternal-natural; by bringing forth from the world of femininity reflections, hypotheses which are necessarily ruinous for the bastion which still holds the authority. (441)

Third World feminism employs the concept of alterity, which means other, to theorise about the position of the subaltern. The term **subaltern** refers to oppressed, marginalised or colonised individuals and communities, in other words individuals who have been radically othered through **colonialism**. Third World feminist **Gayatri Chakravorty Spivak** asks the question 'Can the subaltern speak?' (283) in her 1988 article 'Can the Subaltern Speak?' Her response to this question is 'the subaltern cannot speak' (308) because the subaltern woman is effectively silenced by the theorist that is claiming to speak for her. Thus the subaltern woman is further othered by those claiming to be speaking for her.

Ecofeminists have argued that western culture treats non-human nature as Other. Ecofeminist **Val Plumwood** in her 1994 book *Feminism and the Mastery of Nature* connects **dualisms** to othering. She argues that viewing humans and nature as separate and opposed and clinging to Cartesian **rationality** has led to a distancing of humans from nature and a ruthless treatment of nature as Other. In turn, this has led to pervasive environmental destruction and a denigration of all non-human life as well as humans that are cultural others – women of all colours and non-white men and children.

Outsider-within: a term first used by **Patricia Hill Collins** in her 1986 article 'Learning from the Outsider Within: The Sociological Significance of Black Feminist Thought' to describe the type of knowledge and positioning African-American women developed through domestic work in white households. As outsiders working within privileged white households Black women were able to have a view into **whiteness** and white domesticity that not only was not afforded to other Blacks, but also was not critically understood by whites. But because these women were Black, they never could be fully within the white household; they thus were always outside, positioned on the margins 'between groups of varying power' (Collins, 1998: 5).

In her later work *Fighting Words: Black Women and the Search for Justice* (1998) Collins 'revisits' her 'Learning from the Outsider Within' and provides a revised description of outsider-within. Collins uses the term to indicate social positionings filled with contradictions occupied by groups with unequal power (5). Collins argues that the outsider-within epistemological position is different from oppositional theorising that initiates from positions of power or from theorising through a position focused on only one form of oppression. Theorising as an outsider-within 'reflects the multiplicity of being on the margins with intersecting systems of race, class, gender, sexual, and national oppression, even as such theory remains grounded in and attentive to real differences in power' (8).

Outsider-within has been a useful theoretical and practical term for many areas of feminist philosophy, including but not limited to **decolonisation** and women's positioning in the sciences.

P

Pateman, Carole: white British-born US feminist political scientist. Carole Pateman is the author of two books that have been highly influential in feminist social and political philosophy: *The Disorder of Women* (1990) and *The Sexual Contract* (1988). In *The Sexual Contract* Pateman argues that the social contract, which serves as the foundation for western democracy and is taken by mainstream political theorists to be a contract that is built on and sustains equality and rights, is really a sexual contract, in other words 'political right as *patriarchal right* or sex-right, the power that men exercise over women' (1). This sexual contract permeates the institutional public order as well as private daily life. Since the social contract is really a sexual contract women are never beneficiaries of the contract, thus women are never really protected by contractarian rights and are never free individuals. In the *Disorder of Women* Pateman argues that women are viewed under **patriarchal** models as disordered on two counts. First, just being a woman is a disorder itself. With man as the norm, woman is inherently disordered, lacking the **objectivity, rationality** and neutrality **embodied** in masculinity. Second, because women are disordered, they create disorder and thus must be kept out of the political realm. Pateman uses the work of major social contract theorists such as Locke and Hobbes to trace her arguments into contemporary western social contract democracies.

Patriarchy: patriarchy literally means 'father rule'. In practice it is the institutionalisation and legitimation of sexism (hooks, 2000). Patriarchy is the systemisation of the **oppression** of women by social structures such as marriage, heterosexuality, laws, policies and even language. Feminists have written about, analysed and fought against patriarchy on numerous levels. For example, feminist political theorist Carol Pateman argues in *The Sexual Contract* (1988) that the social contract, which is the foundation for western democracy, is really a sexual contract, in other words 'political right as *patriarchal right* or sexright, the power that men exercise over women' (1). **Luce Irigaray** in *This Sex Which Is Not One* (1985a) points to the patriarchal nature of psychoanalytic theory. She argues that in psychoanalytic theory the *'feminine occurs only within models and laws devised by male subjects'* (86). The discourse generated from this perspective is circular and thus makes writing on female pleasure 'often prematurely emitted, makes him miss... what her own pleasure might be all about' (91). Arguments for **reproductive rights**, protection against violence and the right to same-sex marriages have all been fights against patriarchy.

Performativity: feminist **queer theorist Judith Butler** utilises performativity to theorise the 'doing of gender' as a way to understand subjectivity. In her book *Gender Trouble* (1990) Butler argues that *'gender* is not a noun, neither is it a set of free-floating attributes... gender is performativity produced and compelled by the regulatory practices of gender coherence. Gender is always doing...' Furthermore, gender identity is the expression of performing gender and nothing more than this (25). Butler makes clear in her preface to *Bodies that Matter* (1994) that gender is not performed in the sense of something that is donned every morning. Gender is not intentional in that wilful sense. Gender is something that is put on a body by the materiality of its existence. One performs gender as society expects that repetitious, ritualised performance (x). In this text Butler describes performativity as citationality. Butler states 'the norm of sex takes hold to the extent that it is "cited" as such a norm, but it also derives its power through the citations that it compels' (13). It is a repetition of a norm that is so **hegemonic** that it only needs reference to itself for justification and continued repetition and neither the repetition nor the justification is noticed.

Phallocentric/phallocratic: a term used in feminist theory to indicate the cultural centrality of male experience and the primacy of the male phallus/penis. Feminists have pointed to numerous and different types of phallocentrism in western culture. Just a few examples are the use of the 'man' to stand as a neutral placeholder for both male and female and the view of philosophical argumentation as a verbal sword fight. French psychoanalyst Jacques Lacan originally used the term to refer to the **symbolic** order that privileges masculinity over femininity. In 'Sortics' [1986] (1999) **Hélène Cixous** says '[p]hallocentricism *is*. History has never produced, recorded anything but that . . . Phallocentricism is the enemy. Of *everyone*. Men stand to lose by it, differently but as seriously as women. And it is time to transform. To invent the other history' (441).

See **androcentric; masculinist**

Plumwood, Val: white Australian ecofeminist philosopher. Val Plumwood's 1994 book *Feminism and the Mastery of Nature* locates the destruction of the non-human world in the western obsession with **dualisms**. Viewing humans and nature as separate and opposed and clinging to Cartesian **rationality** has led to a distancing of humans from nature and a ruthless treatment of nature as **Other**. This further masks our human dependency on nature and creates a false sense of human autonomy.

In *Environmental Culture: The Ecological Crisis of Reason* (2002) Plumwood extends this argument, claiming that western culture's obsession with rationality is not only irrational, but what masquerades as rationality is itself irrational and has led to our current ecological and social crisis. She states that the 'ecological crisis is the crisis of a cultural "mind" that cannot acknowledge and adapt itself properly to its material "body", the embodied and ecological support base it draws on in the long-denied counter-sphere of "nature"' (15). Plumwood seeks to 'situate non-humans ethically' (2), recognising nature's **agency**, and to situate humans in ecological terms, thus breaking down the human/nature dualism. She ultimately uses a revised version of deep ecology, one that understands nature as an active agent and humans and non-humans as part of a continuum to argue against the pervasive Lockean views of private property that are generated by the rationalist, dualist approach taken by western thinking. She argues for a model of partnership with non-humans and other humans that is cooperative, responsive and mutual in which '[b]asic decision power in the land could be vested more broadly in larger continuing publics, who might represent nature politically via a system of accountability to trustees and speakers for particular places and for larger ecological systems including biospheric nature' (217).

See **ecofeminism; Warren, Karen**

Pluralism: the view that many different ideas and knowers coming together make better social, political, ethical and epistemological decisions. **Donna Haraway** in her essay 'Situated Knowledges: The Science Question in Feminism and the Privilege of Partial Perspectives' in *Simians, Cyborgs and Women* (1991) argues that an **embodied, situated knowledge** generated from a plurality of perspectives will provide greater objectivity in the sciences. Each perspective is local, particular, gendered, raced and classed and results in a particular vision or perspective. All perspectives are partial and the plurality of them joined together provides a better chance of reaching objectivity.

The understanding of plurality in the above sense is an instrumental understanding; that is, pluralism is valued because it can be used to achieve something else, in this case objectivity and knowledge. Pluralism can also have intrinsic value; that is, it is valued just because it is important to value the presence of a variety of different perspectives, people, theories, methodologies, simply for the sake that each of these is important and deserving of recognition in and of itself. A contrast to both the intrinsic and instrumental understandings of pluralism is the existence of **monocultures**. Monocultures, whether physical or epistemological, take pluralism to be a threat because monocultures are predicated on a lack of diversity. For example, **Sandra Harding** argues that the lack of pluralism in the sciences results in an epistemic **monoculture**; in other words, it results in a homogeneity of knowledge that appears to be objective and value-neutral, but is value-laden. She argues that the problem 'is not that individuals in the community are androcentric, Eurocentric or economically overprivileged (though that certainly doesn't help)' (1992: 579), but that within this dominant discourse certain methodologies and modes of research have been made to appear to be normal/natural and unassailable and alternative views that would create a pluralism are kept out. Thus a lack of pluralism of people leads to an epistemic monoculture.

Maria Lugones in her essay 'On the Logic of Pluralist Feminism' (1991) articulates the dangers for **women of colour** when feminist theory is not intentionally pluralist. Her writing exhibits the pluralism that she is arguing for and the pain and danger that she is working to articulate. Lugones says:

When I do not see plurality stressed in the very structure of a theory, I know that I will have to do lots of acrobatics – like a contortionist or tight-rope walker – to have this theory speak to me without allowing the theory to distort me *in my complexity*. When I do not see plurality in the very structure of a theory, I see the phantom that I am in your eyes take grotesque forms and mime crudely and heavily your own image. Don't you? When I do not see pluralism in the very structure of a theory, I see the fool that I am mimicking your image for the pleasure of notic- ing that you know no better. Don't you? When I do not see plurality in the very structure of a theory, I see the woman of color that I am speaking precisely and seriously in calm anger as if trying to shatter thick layers of deafness accompanied by a clear sense of my own absurdity. Don't you? When I do not see plu- rality in the very structure of a theory, I see myself in my all-raza women's group in the church basement in Arroyo Seco, Nuevo Mejico, suddenly struck dumb, the theoretical words asphyxiating me. Don't you? When you do not see plurality in the very structure of a theory, what do you see? (43)

Lugones articulates the diminishing, distorting and **oth- ering** that results from non-pluralistic theories that speak for and appropriate, or speak without understanding, other women's experiences.

Luce Irigarary in *This Sex Which Is Not One* (1985a) also emphasises the importance of pluralism, taking this pluralism to be embodied and through **embodiment** conncctcd to thcory and practice. Irigaray suggests that women can create their own feminine sexuality, one that is plural, modelled on their own sexual organs, the labia that are already two and maybe more, and their own orgasms as multiple. She states '[h]er sexuality is at least double, goes even further; it is plural' (1985a: 32). Just as the **phallocentric** order translates from sexuality through to language and theory, so does female sexuality. Feminine theory, language, and social order will thus be multiple and pluralistic.

Criticisms and insights from all branches of feminist philosophy and from numerous thinkers, including Lugones, Harding, Haraway and Luce Irigaray, have made clear the importance of pluralism in feminist theory and practice.

Further reading: Harding (1991, 1998); Lugones (1987, 2003); Shiva (1993, 1997)

Polyversal: in her 2001 book *Manmade Breast Cancers* Zillah Eisenstein uses the word 'polyversal' in contrast to **universal** to recognise the **pluralism** of women's experiences while at the same time recognising a sharedness among women. Eisenstein describes polyversal in the following way:

> *Poly-* means many or diverse. *Versal* is shorthand for designating the whole or the entirety of a thing. Together they embrace the universality of humanity while demanding an earnest specifying of its different meanings; hence, *poly-* replaces *uni-*. This requires the deep belief that I can really learn from experiences that are not my own. (151)

She connects the term to the projects of **anti-racist feminism** and **transnational feminism** as well as **anti-capitalist critiques.**

Postcolonial Feminism: **Ofelia Schutte** describes postcolonial feminism as

> those feminisms that take the experience of Western colonialism and its contemporary effects as a high priority in the process of setting up a speaking position from which to articulate a standpoint of cultural, national, regional, or social identity. With postcolonial feminisms, the process of critique is turned against the domination and exploitation of *culturally* different others. Postcolonial feminisms differ from the classic critique of imperialism in that they try to stay away from rigid self – other binaries. In addition, an intense criticism is directed at the gender stereotypes and symbolic constructs of the woman's body used to reinforce outdated masculinist notions of national identity. (1998: 65–6)

Thus postcolonial feminists frequently use the tools of the colonisers against them to transform domination and exploitation. Postcolonial feminism generates a theoretical perspective from the **embodied** experiences of those that have been **colonised** both physically and metaphysically. It challenges self–other binaries dominant in western thinking. It works to recognise the differences and to build solidarity among Third World women. Postcolonial feminists attempt to decolonise the colonised subject through 'an active withdrawal of consent and resistance to the structure of psychic and social domination' and results in a radical transformation of social structures and individual and collective identity (Mohanty,

2003: 7–8). Postcolonial feminists critique capitalism's corporatisation of daily life across the globe, the marketing of the colonised other and the exploitation of the labour of Third World women as well as analyse the intersection of gender and national identity and gender and development.

See **anti-capitalist critique; anti-racist feminism; colonisation; decolonisation; Mohanty, Chandra Talpade; Third World feminism**

Postfeminism: the term postfeminist has two meanings. The first is the popular press usage to indicate that feminism, particularly **second wave feminism**, is dead and that we've moved into a mode in which women want the benefits that came with feminism, but still dress, act and do as they please even if it replicates **patriarchal** gender norms. The second meaning of the term comes from the extension of anti-essentialist arguments in **postmodern feminism**. If the term 'woman' is **socially constructed** and women's experiences are divergent and different, then the unity and sameness that feminism rested upon does not exist. In addition, many postfeminists see postfeminism as the logical outgrowth of feminism and as connected to other 'post' projects. Ann Brooks in *Postfeminisms* (1997) states:

> The term is now understood as a useful conceptual frame of reference encompassing the intersection of feminism, poststructuralism and postcolonialism. Postfeminism represents feminism's 'coming of age,' its maturity into a confident body of theory and politics, representing pluralism and difference and reflecting on its position in relation to other philosophical and political movements similarly demanding change. (1)

There have been numerous arguments against postfeminism. Some feminists are concerned that the theoretical use of the term, the second usage of it, will be conflated with the media usage of the term, thus pushing back social strides that women have made and glorifying the use of women's bodies as entertainment for men. Other feminists have argued that what postfeminism claims to do – value the pluralism of women's experiences – is already being done in feminism without losing the strategy of seeking connections among women. For example, **Third Wave feminism, transnational feminism, anti-racist feminism** and **postcolonial feminism,** as well as the reflective work of many second wave feminists, are areas of feminism that seek pluralism and connection.

Postmodern feminism: originating in France in the 1970s with the work of **Hélène Cixous, Julia Kristeva** and **Luce Irigaray,** postmodern feminism has had significant influence on feminist philosophy passed the turn of the twenty-first century whether it has been through critical negative reactions to its theoretical underpinnings, adoption of it as a theoretical approach or the use of specific theoretical elements. Postmodern feminism is heavily influenced by the work of **Simone de Beauvoir,** Jacques Derrida and Jacques Lacan. It has emphasised the plurality of women's experiences, has resisted defining 'woman', 'women' and 'feminine', is anti-**essentialist,** is critical of **dualisms** and seeks to understand **embodied** experience. Postmodern feminism furthers Derrida's 'difference' to understand it as a positive positioning that can help to understand how women's different experiences, resulting from race, class, ethnicity, ability, sexuality and age, lead to different social positioning, different knowledge claims and different ways of being.

Postmodern feminism has been criticised as being overly theoretical, politically dangerous to feminism in its unwillingness to theorise a category 'woman' and not politically useful by not focusing on practical aspects of women's oppression or on liberatory struggles (Tong, 1998). Many postmodern feminists would argue against these criticisms. For example, Susan Bordo in *Unbearable Weight* (1993) uses a postmodern approach to analyse the tyranny that contemporary media and advertising has over women's perceptions and experiences of their bodies. She argues that postmodern analysis can help us to read how the body is made to be text and teaches us to read advertising such that we come to understand how we embody messages. Through this critical lens women can learn to resist the pull of cultural messages about their bodies. Furthermore, even though postmodern feminists may be unwilling to provide a fixed definition of 'woman' or 'women', it is evident from their work, such as Hélène Cixous's *écriture féminine*, 'women's writing', and Luce Irigaray's *The Sex Which Is Not One* (1985a) in which she argues for the pluralistic nature of being a woman, that they are theorising about women and have a working concept of 'woman'.

Potter, Elizabeth: white US feminist philosopher specialising in philosophy of science and epistemology. Potter is a co-editor of one of the first readers on **feminist epistemology** *Feminist Epistemologies* (1993) as well as the author of *Gender and Boyle's Law of Gases* (2001). With this book Potter provides a gender and class analysis of theory choice in early seventeenth-century science. Potter uses Boyle's Law as an example of science that is taken to be mathematically pure, good science, but is instead is riddled with **background assumptions**. Potter points to the economic, political and gendered background assumptions and biases which influenced Boyle's theory choice. Among them are Boyle's apparent resentment of his mother, his fear of loose women, his concern about the monarchy and his strong aversion to animist views of nature.

Pragmatist feminism: in *Pragmatism and Feminism* (1996) **Charlene Haddock Seigfried** develops the first succinct definition of pragmatist feminism. Seigfried argues that pragmatism and feminism have much in common and much to learn from each other, thus making for a fruitful and insightful theoretical approach and practical methodology. They both seek to include diverse and **marginalised** communities, seeking a **pluralism** of views. They reject the separation of ethics and epistemology, the idea of a neutral, **objective** observer. Both tend to be anti-**essentialist** though may employ **strategic essentialism**, and both make an explicit connection between theory and practice, and recognise the importance of critical revision and reshaping of ideas and practices.

> Pragmatism and feminism reject philosophizing as an intellectual game that takes purely logical analysis as its special task. For both, philosophy is a means, not ends. The specific, practical ends are set by various communities of interest, the members of which are best situated to name, resist, and overcome oppressions of class, sex, race, and gender. (37)

Seigfried argues that pragmatism can learn from feminism's explicit locating of women as a marginalised subject with a unique frame of reference from which to start thinking and practice. Because pragmatists assume women come under a blanket category of oppressed groups and do 'not actually reflect on the status of women and the oppressions of race, class, sexual orientation, and economic forces that women suffer, they are contributing to the justification of the established order' (38).

Feminism can also benefit from pragmatism's insights, according to Seigfried, by recognising pragmatism's radical 'revisions of the task of philosophy' to move outside its narrow disciplinary context by recognising this context and embracing the context of everyday life. Seigfried asserts that '[p]ragmatist feminists and feminist pragmatists exist among us, but in surprisingly small numbers . . . This is a loss for both pragmatist and feminist theory and praxis' (39).

Further reading: Sullivan (2001)

Probyn, Elspeth: white Australian gender theorist specialising in media studies, food, bodies and sexuality. Probyn studies the manifestation of identity/ies in many facets of daily life. In *Sexing the Self* (1993), Probyn argues that the sexed self or the gendered self has been insufficiently studied in feminist theory. The self 'designates a *combinatoire*, a discursive arrangement that holds together in tension the different lines of race and sexuality that form and re-from our senses of self' (1–2). Probyn argues that through rethinking the sexed self feminists can explore how it can be a driving force in generating new theoretical and practical positions in feminist theory. Probyn describes the bulk of her writing as projects that work through her preoccupations with her own self. Her work is particularly engaged with daily life and because of this she is a public figure in Australian media. Her other books include *Outside Belongings* (1996), *Carnal Appetites: FoodSexIdentities* (2000) and *Blush: Faces of Shame* (2005).

See **feminist aesthetics; gender; race**

Prochoice: prochoice is the view that women should be able to choose whether or not to have a child. It follows from this choice that women should have the right to have legal, safe and practical access to abortion. Prochoice arguments support abortion rights on several fronts, such as the right to privacy and integrity of one's body as provided by the *Roe* v. *Wade* ruling in 1973 in the US and the Abortion Act 1967 in the UK, the non-personhood status of a foetus (Warren, 2000), and foetal dependency on a women's body (Thomson, 1971). Some African-American feminists such as **bell hooks** argue that the term prochoice should be applied not only to the right to have an abortion, but that it should also include the right to choose to have a child, the right to not be sterilised and the right to birth control (2000).

Public/Private Distinction: in liberal political theory the public has been defined not only as that aspect of life that is subject to view by others, but it is also that aspect that is subject to the view of the state and thus subject to political discussion, state regulation and community modification. The private is that aspect of life that is not subject to the view of the state and community and should be protected from the state and the community. Traditionally the home and the body are given as examples of the private realm. Because the body has been part of the private realm, abortion rights groups, as well as the *Roe* v. *Wade* ruling in the US and the Abortion Act 1967 in the UK, have argued that a women's right to choose to have an abortion is part of her private moral decision-making and part of her right to bodily integrity that cannot be infringed upon by the public realm of the state. Groups opposed to abortion have argued that a foetus's public right to be protected by the state supersedes a woman's private right to choose to have an abortion. On the other hand, certain aspects of life have been forced out of the public realm and into the private. For example, for centuries domestic violence was considered to be out the realm of state regulation because by its very definition, as domestic, it was private. Thus a husband's or a parent's right to privately abuse one's wife or child was, in effect, protected by the public/private distinction. Many aspects of women's daily lives, especially those that are bodily, such as breastfeeding, have been socially condemned and thus relegated to the home, effectively keeping women domesticated.

The public/private distinction is a **dualism** that many feminists have critiqued and analysed. The public has been aligned with masculine, **rationality**, **objectivity** and **universal** and the private with feminine, emotion, subjectivity and particular. In most cases, feminists have not argued for abolishing the distinction between public and private, but have instead argued that the distinction is not as clear as it is made to appear and that how these categories are defined needs to be rethought. For example, **Iris Marion Young** in *Justice and the Politics of Difference* (1990) argues for a reconceptualisation of these realms, though not an abolition of the distinction. She argues for a heterogeneous understanding of public life that recognises and respects differences instead of prioritising and seeking universal characteristics. Young states:

> Instead of defining the private as what the public excludes, I suggest that the private should be defined, as in one strain of liberal theory, as that aspect of his or her life and activity that any person has a right to exclude others from. The private in this sense is not what public institutions exclude, but what the individual chooses to withdrawal from public view... This manner of formulating the concepts of public and private... does not deny their

distinction. It does deny, however, a social division between public and private spheres, each with different kinds of institutions, activities, and human attributes. The concept of a heterogeneous public implies two political principles: (a) no persons, actions, or aspects of a person's life should be forced into privacy; and (b) no social institutions or practices should be excluded a priori from being a proper subject for public discussion and expression. (120)

Young uses this distinction to argue that such issues as **sexuality**, which is traditionally taken to be private and hidden from the public realm, thus closeting lesbians, gays and transgendered people and excluding them from public life, should not be forced in to privacy if individuals wish to be visible.

Q

Queer theory: queer theory originated in gay and lesbian studies in the 1990s. Though by its very subject matter it is intentionally difficult to define, Annamarie Jagose in *Queer Theory: An Introduction* (1997) describes queer theory as a theoretical perspective that ruptures traditional models of academic discourse (3):

[It] describes those gestures or analytic models which dramatize incoherencies in the allegedly stable relations between chromosomal sex, gender and sexual desire. Resisting the model of stability – which claims heterosexuality as its origin, when it is more properly its effect – queer focuses on the mismatch between sex, gender and desire. (3)

In feminist philosophy **Judith Butler** is the most well recognised queer theorist. Her book *Gender Trouble* (1990) has not only served as a foundational text in queer theory, it has evoked a substantial amount of discussion and criticism in queer theory and feminist theory. Butler argues in her book *Undoing Gender* (2004) that 'queer theory is understood, by definition, to oppose all identity claims, including sex assignment' (7). Some feminists worry that queer theory is dangerous for feminist theory because they claim it makes it difficult to study women and gender as analytical categories.

See **essentialism; gender and sex; social construction**

R

Race: race theorists Michael Omi and Howard Winant in their book *Racial Formation in the United States* (1994) define race as 'a concept which signifies and symbolizes social conflicts and interests by referring to different types of human bodies' (55). They point out that even though race is socially attached to particular bodies, that is particular phenotypes, there is no biological basis for race. Thus race is a complex, socially mediated construct that orders society, marginalises people and is used to justify economic, educational and medical inequalities.

Linda Martín Alcoff argues in her book *Visible Identities: Race, Gender and the Self* (2006) that 'race works through the domain of the visible, the experience of race is predicated first and foremost on the perception of race, a perception whose specific mode is a learned ability' (187). Alcoff is arguing that we learn to see race and we learn to live as racial beings. Thus race becomes a way of seeing and a way of being.

Feminists of colour have theorised about the intersection of race and **gender** since the beginnings of **second wave feminism**, but white feminists were slower to do so. In 'I Am Your Sister: Black Women Organizing Across Sexualities' (1990), Black lesbian feminist **Audre Lorde** describes how the intertwined affects of **racism** and homophobia keep Black women from organising. She states

> [h]omophobia and heterosexism mean you allow yourself to be robbed of the sisterhood and strength of Black Lesbian women because you are afraid of being called a Lesbian yourself. Yet we share many of the concerns as Black women, so much work to be done. The urgency of the destruction of our black children and the theft of young Black minds are joint urgencies. (324)

Furthermore, white feminists were slow to recognise racism in feminism itself and unclear on how to constructively work through it. For example, Chela Sandoval in her report 'Feminism and Racism: A Report on the 1981 National Women's Studies Association' (1990) explains that in the initial attempts to respond to racism, white feminists replicated the racism that they thought they were acknowledging by creating a hierarchical structure to the conference, not allowing time to think and reflect on racism and by making the conference prohibitively expensive for many **women of colour** who, because of racism in the academy, were not in academic positions and were unable to afford the conference fee.

See **biological determinism; essentialism; oppression**

Racism: in the most basic sense, racism is a type of **oppression** in which one **race** is valued over others, actively or passively. This most basic sense does not capture the complexity or the insidious nature of racism. Racism is a structural, **embodied** hatred of others that results in economic, social and educational disparities, emotional damage, wars, **colonisation** and death. **María Lugones** in her essay 'Hablando cara a cara/Speaking face to face: An Exploration of Ethnocentric Racism' (1990) defines racism as

> one's affirmation of or acquiescence to or lack of recognition of the structures and mechanisms of the racial state; one's lack of awareness of or blindness or indifference to one's being racialized; one's affirmation of, indifference or blindness to the harm that the racist state inflicts on some of its members. (49)

Linda Martín Alcoff defines racism as 'a negative value or set of values projected as an essential attribute onto a group whose members are defined through genealogical connection, sharing some origin, and who are demarcated on the basis of some visible features' (2006: 259). By this Alcoff means that racists mark certain undesirable attributes – physical and behavioural – as fixed, natural traits of a person that connects them to a group with which they share some relation.

Radical feminism: radical feminism evolved out of the women's liberation movement of the 1960s. Like **socialist feminists**, radical feminists argued that new political, economic and social categories needed to be constructed to end the **patriarchy's oppression** of women. Radical feminism is marked by at least three commitments:

1. The struggle to end the oppression of women should take priority over ending other forms of oppression because gender oppression is the cause of all other forms of oppression and is more widespread than any other (Jaggar, 1988).

2. Gender oppression is an unquestioned, invisible, framework functioning at all levels in patriarchal society.
3. Institutionalized heterosexuality is the root of patriarchy's control of women.

There are libertarian and cultural strains to radical feminism. Libertarian-radical feminism points to the sex/gender system – the process of making social constructions of gender appear to be biological, fixed and purely sexed based – is used by patriarchy to keep women passive, disempowered and subservient to men. Thus one part of ending the oppression of women is to break the sex/gender system and to recognise that 'women are no more destined to be passive than men are destined to be active' (Tong, 1998: 49). Some libertarian radical feminists argue that androgyny through the elimination of gender is the best means to achieve this goal, for example Kate Millet (1970); others argue that women's reproductive and nurturative role is the cause of their oppression and that technology that will end women's need to be reproductive vessels and new social structures are needed to free women, for example **Shulamith Firestone** (1970); and others argue that the norms of heterosexuality subordinate, divide and make women invisible and that becoming a lesbian is to work to end women's oppression, for example **Marilyn Frye** (1984). Cultural-radical feminists extol womanhood and feminine characteristics that are constructed free from patriarchy (Jaggar, 1988) and point toward an essential female nature that should be celebrated and not muddied with masculine traits and ideals, for example **Mary Daly** (1978).

Rationality: rationality is a value of western thought that consists in the individual's capacity to distance of him or herself from the subject and is believed to result in objective, value-neutral decision-making. Feminists have analysed and critiqued rationality on a number of fronts. One of the most common criticisms of rationality is that it is **androcentric**. What results from this claim varies among feminists. For example, **liberal feminists** don't necessarily think that rationality itself is a problem, but believe that the model of rationality as 'the rational man' is problematic. The challenge then would be to make a conception of rationality that is gender-neutral. Other feminists think that the concept of rationality is so androcentric that it is useless to feminist theory. For example, in 'The Laugh of Medusa' [1975] (1983) **Hélène Cixous** uses the term *écriture féminine*, women's writing, to describe an embodied writing by women that is antithetical to androcentric rationality. *Ecriture féminine* approaches its subject through desire, subjectivity and emotion instead of through static, lifeless rationality.

Some feminists have also argued that rationality is **Eurocentric**. For example, **Chicana feminist Gloria Anzaldúa** argues in *Borderlands/La Frontera* (1987) that the *new mestiza consciousness* embodies both the values of Anglo and Indian culture. She says:

> *La Mestiza* constantly has to shift out of habitual formations; from convergent, analytical thinking that tends to use rationality to move toward a single goal (a Western mode) to divergent thinking, characterized by movement away from set patterns and goals and toward a more whole perspective, one that includes rather than excludes. (101)

Another area of feminist philosophy that has provided critiques of rationality is **ecofeminism.** Ecofeminists have argued that clinging to rationality has been destructive to the human and non-human world. For example, **Val Plumwood** argues in *Environmental Culture: The Ecological Crisis of Reason* (2002) that western culture's obsession with rationality is not only irrational, but what masquerades as rationality is itself irrational and has led to our current ecological and social crisis. She states that the 'ecological crisis is the crisis of a cultural "mind" that cannot acknowledge and adapt itself properly to its material "body", the embodied and ecological support base it draws on in the long-denied counter-sphere of "nature" ' (15).

See **objectivity**

Reason: see **rationality**

Reflexivity: reflexivity has become a highly valued intellectual tool in **feminist science studies, feminist epistemology** and **postcolonial feminism**. In most literature arguing for a more reflexive approach, reflexivity is characterised as developing a more critical consciousness through reflection upon one's epistemological location. An epistemological location consists of the belief framework from which one holds conceptual, historical and political commitments. Reflexivity, then, consists of acknowledging, critically evaluating and publicly recognising one's epistemological location. Valuing reflexivity has encouraged some feminist science critics to approach their own work reflexively and to argue for a greater level of reflexivity in the sciences. **Sandra Harding**'s *Is Science Multicultural?* (1998) is an example of reflexivity in practice. Harding continually locates herself in the text and assesses her position and the position of the knowledge developed out of the western framework in which she has participated. Harding asks such questions as 'What is the social location of this study . . . and what is its epistemological stance?' (188). She locates her study as originating in the North at

> a particular moment and site of northern discourses. It draws upon the historical and cultural legacies of those cultures – for example European and European feminist social theories, postcolonialism as articulated in a certain range of English-language writings, histories, sociologies, ethnographies, and philosophies of sciences as these are produced and debated in Europe and the United States, and so forth. (191)

Harding works at problematising her location, making clear that any location is a chaotic, yet informative, space. Both Sandra Harding and **Donna Haraway** build upon this basic conception of reflexivity. Harding terms her version **strategic/robust reflexivity** (1998) or **strong reflexivity** (1991) while Haraway does away with the term reflexivity and adopts the alternative label of **diffraction** (1997).

Reproductive Rights: reproductive rights encompass a broad array of rights tied to women and reproduction. Though people tend to think mostly about the right to have an abortion that was established by the *Roe* v. *Wade* ruling in 1973 in the US and the Abortion Act 1967 in the UK, reproductive rights extend much farther than this and should be understood as a global concern, not just a local US and UK issue. Among the rights feminists seek to address are the following:

1. The right to adequate health care and maternity care. For example, women should have affordable or free access to mammograms and prenatal and neonatal care.

2. The right to choose to have a child. For example, poor white women and women of colour, regardless of economics, are socially stigmatised and disadvantaged for having children; lesbians have had courts take their children taken from them; women in some Third World countries are socially and materially ostracized for not having children.

3. The right to affordable and easy access to birth control and protection from HIV. For example, the US's Mexico City Policy, an anti-abortion policy that keeps US aid from worldwide clinics that are associated with abortion, has caused the closing of clinics, a shortage of condoms to help prevent the spread of HIV, and a loss of maternity and neonatal care.

4. The right to not be sterilised or have one's body mutilated. For example, African-American and Native American women were sterilised up to the 1970s and in some countries female genital mutilation is still practised commonly as a way of controlling a women's sexuality.

Feminists have fought politically and written extensively about the importance of reproductive rights. Reproductive rights have not been a category of rights theorised by mainstream, **masculinist** social and political philosophy.

See also **Prochoice**

Further reading: Cudd (2005); Knudsen and Hartmann (2006); Mahowald (2004); Nelson (2003)

Reproductive Technology: modern science and medicine have developed a number of technologies that have become standard in the reproductive care of women and fetuses. Among them are ultrasound, in vitro fertilisation, gender selection, sampling circulating fetal cells, genetic testing and selective abortion. Feminists have a complex relation to reproductive technology. **Shulamith Firestone** argued in *The Dialectic of Sex* (1970) that reproductive technology could free women from **patriarchy,** the burden of female biology and the bearing of children. Robyn Rowland in her 1992 book *Living Laboratories: Women and Reproductive Technologies* argues that the move to more advanced and more sophisticated reproductive technologies increases patriarchal control over women's bodies.

The complexity of the debate in feminist theory regarding reproductive technologies is connected to the issue of **reproductive rights**. Most feminists want women to be able to choose to have an abortion or to have a child and most feminists want women to have control over their bodies, but reproductive technologies such as sampling circulating fetal cells for genetic diseases and gender selection can lead to selective abortion of fetuses. Selective abortion for these reasons can clash with feminists' commitment to valuing and fighting for the rights of people with disabilities and the fight to have female children valued as much as male children, that is fights against ableism and sexism (Silvers, in Silvers et al., 1998; Tremain, 2005). On the other side of this debate, Laura Purdy argues in her 'Genetic Diseases: Can Having Children Be Immoral' (1978) that parents who know that they are pregnant with a fetus with a severe genetic disease or defect have a moral obligation to abort because this future child has the right to a minimally satisfying life.

Race and **class** issues also play a role in reproductive technologies. **Mary Mahowald** argues in *Genes, Women and Equity* (2000) that genetic interventions are not gender, race or class neutral. Women pay a disproportionate burden of the invasive technology that accompanies genetic technology. Furthermore, most genetic reproductive technology benefits white middle- and upper-class, educated women.

Ruddick, Sara: white US feminist philosopher specialising in ethics and social and political philosophy. Ruddick is the author of *Maternal Thinking: Toward a Politics of Peace* (1989) in which she argues that maternal thinking is a 'disciplined reflection' that arises out of the practice of mothering and can be the basis for moral theory and action. Maternal thinking includes learning to think and feel through the eyes of another, conflict resolution, experiencing physical risk, self-sacrifice, **embodiment**, nurturing, creation and the experience of **gender oppression**. Ruddick argues that this is a type of feminist **standpoint epistemology** that can be used as a position from which to generate a more peaceful, cooperative society.

S

Schutte, Ofelia: **Latina feminist** specialising in Latin American and postcolonial feminism, Continental philosophy and philosophy of culture. Written from the perspective of postcolonial feminist theory and with the insights of postmodernism, Schutte's *Cultural Identity and Social Liberation in Latin American Thought* (1993) develops a historical account of *mestizaje* identity, one that is contrasted with the purity that is incessant in European and colonial accounts of identity. Schutte argues that '*mestizaje* [. . .] refers to a combined assimilation of various cultural traditions and today includes a recognition of the importance of the indigenous and African heritages of the people of the region' (241). Through its historical development it is a reciprocal, anticolonial, egalitarian notion of identity that exists in opposition to the individualist, purist, colonialist, hierarchical European concept of identity. Schutte also provides an analysis of the effects of globalisation on female workers, the rise of the women's antiviolence movements, and the Catholic and **patriarchal oppression** of women's sexuality in Latin America.

In her article 'Cross-Cultural Alterity: Cross-Cultural Communication and Feminist Theory in North–South Contexts' (1998), Schutte asks 'Is it possible for contemporary Western feminism to disentangle itself from Western colonialism and from the erasure of otherness that such forces entail?' (65). She provides a nuanced view of postcolonial feminism as:

> those feminisms that take the experience of Western colonialism and its contemporary effects as a high priority in the process of setting up a speaking position from which to articulate a standpoint of cultural, national, regional, or social identity. With postcolonial feminisms, the process of critique is turned against the domination and exploitation of *culturally* different others. Postcolonial feminisms differ from the classic critique of imperialism in that they try to stay away from rigid self-other binaries. In addition, an intense criticism is directed at the gender stereotypes and symbolic contructs of the woman's body used to reinforce outdated masculinist notions of national identity. (1998: 65–6)

Schutte is critical of western feminism's seeming desire to **universalise** and make its agenda the global agenda for all women. Yet she doesn't think western feminism is a lost cause. In answer to whether western feminism can work to move away from colonialism, Schutte does think that feminism can attempt to disentangle itself. It can do so by working to adopt a postcolonial feminism. She argues that '[f]eminist ethical thinking needs to be "negotiated" cross-culturally', either case by case or collectively, recognising the particularities and insights of culturally marginalised people (68).

Schutte is also the author of *Beyond Nihilism: Nietzsche without Masks* (1984), with a Spanish translation in 2000, *Más allá del nihilismo: Nietzsche sin máscaras* by Eloy Rodríguez Navarro.

Second Wave Feminism: the feminist movement, sometimes called the 'Women's Movement', that began in the late 1960s. In the US it was influenced by the strategies and tactics of the Civil Rights movement and in the UK by the labour rights movement. The phrase 'the personal is the political' became a rallying cry in the movement to argue for such things as the right to an abortion and equal pay for equal work. Furthermore 'the personal is the political' made clear that domesticity, marriage and gender norms were political, reflecting social values that were made to appear to be biological givens.

Women's bodies became sites of political contest as the right to bodily integrity and self-determination became focal points of second wave feminism. The UK Abortion Act in 1967 and the 1973 US ruling in *Roe* v. *Wade* giving women the right to have safe, legal abortions were important moments in second wave feminism. Anti-sexual assault and domestic violence campaigns made even more apparent the ways in which the personal is political. Feminists revealed that home and social life can be an inherently dangerous place for many women when the state will not take measures to contest the legality of domestic violence and continues to view rape as a crime to be hidden. Some feminists, such as Adrian Rich and Catherine MacKinnon, argued that, given women's social status, there is no heterosexual intercourse that is truly consensual and free from violence and coercion, that is there is no heterosexual intercourse that is not rape.

Consciousness raising groups were prominent in the 1970s with women gathering to talk and assess their experiences as women. Betty Friedan's *The Feminine Mystique* (1963) became a bestselling book theorising about the lives of middle-class US women. Friedan identified what she called 'the problem that has no name' as the mental and emotional state of educated middle-class housewives tied to home and domesticity.

Though in both the UK and the US pay equity was also an important rallying point, in the US it was largely focused on the work of middle-class women and 'white-collar' workers, while in the UK with the strike at the Ford plant in 1968 the focus extended to working-class women.

The personal was also theorised by feminists who began to question **heternormativity** and **sexuality**. This was one of the first spaces in which lesbian identity began to be addressed in a more public fashion as well as theorised about, though for many feminists sexuality was viewed as an issue that took the movement away from its 'real' focus.

Criticisms of second wave feminism have noted its largely heterosexual, middle-class and white focus. Especially in the US movement, feminists were not especially concerned with working-class labour issues. In both the US and UK feminists frequently treated the concerns of Black women and lesbians as divisive to the movement instead of an important rallying point.

Academic feminism developed from second wave feminism, with many of its early thinkers active in the movement.

Further reading: Nicholson (1997)

Seigfried, Charlene Haddock: white US feminist philosopher specialising in pragmatism and American philosophy.

In 1996 Seigfried published *Pragmatism and Feminism: Reweaving the Social Fabric*, the first systematic analysis of the intersections of feminist theory and practice with early twentieth-century pragmatism. Seigfried works critically through the work and lives of Charlotte Perkins Gilman, Jane Addams, Elsie Ripley Clapp and Ella Flagg Young, situating them within the rise of pragmatism and the history of philosophy. Seigfried draws significant comparisons between the goals and methods of feminism and pragmatism arguing for the importance of feminism for pragmatism and the importance of pragmatism for feminism. She develops a **pragmatist feminism** based on the conjoined insights of feminism and pragmatism. This approach includes valuing and employing the knowledge and experiences of diverse and **marginalised** communities, a **pluralism** of views, a rejection of the separation of ethics and epistemology, and a rejection of the idea of a neutral, **objective** observer. Furthermore, pragmatist feminism recognises that 'specific, practical ends are set by various communities of interest, the members of which are best situated to name, resist, and overcome oppressions of class, sex, race, and gender' (37), and locates women as a marginalised subject with a unique frame of reference from which to start thinking and practice. Since the publication of her book there has been a burgeoning interest in pragmatist approaches.

Semiotic: feminist postmodernist **Julia Kristeva** defines the semiotic as one of two elements of language (the other is the **symbolic**). The semiotic is the rhythm and tone of language through which 'bodily drives are *discharged*' (Kristeva and Oliver, 1997: xiv). The semiotic are the 'meaningful parts of language and yet do not represent or signify something' (Kristeva and Oliver, 1997: xiv). It is the part of language that is non-linguistic,

embodied and is the result of the bodily need to communicate. In her essay 'Revolution in Poetic Language' Kristeva describes the semiotic 'as a psychosomatic modality of the signifying process; in other words, not a symbolic modality but one articulating (in the largest sense of the word) a continuum: the connections between the (glottal and anal) sphincters in (rhythmic and intonational) vocal modulations . . .' (Kristeva and Oliver, 1997: 38). Kristeva argues that genetics, family lineage and all biological constraints, including gender, are part of the semiotic. Because of this and language's dual dependency on the semiotic and symbolic, language reflects the embodiment (gender, genetics, family structures, etc.) that constitutes a person.

Further reading: Kristeva (1980); Kristeva and Oliver (1997)

Separatism: because of the oppressive nature of **patriarchal** culture, some **radical feminists** in the 1970s argued for physically separating themselves from men and establishing feminist communities. For example, theorist and artist Kate Millett established a women-only writer and artist community called the Women's Art Colony Farm. **Marilyn Frye** in her essay 'On Separatism and Power' (1983) describes separatism as 'separation of various sorts or modes from men and from institutions, relationships, roles and activities, which are male-defined, male-dominated and operating for the benefit of males and the maintenance of male privilege – this separatism being initiated or maintained, at will, *by women*' (96).

Some feminists have argued for a metaphysical, instead of a physical, separation from men and patriarchy. For example, in *Lesbian Ethics* (1989) Sarah Hoagland argues for lesbians to choose a value system that is meaningful to them outside of heterosexual, patriarchal norms and withdraw 'from the heterosexual value system' (461). Furthermore, *écriture féminine*, women's writing, a term first used by **Hélène Cixous**, is a type theoretical separatism that indicates writing that is antithetical to **masculinist**, linear, representationalist writing. Cixous argues that masculine writing is static, **disembodied** and free of desire. Feminine writing is where change can take place. 'Women must write her self: must write about women and bring women to writing, from which they have been driven away as violently from their own bodies . . .' (Cixous, 1975: 279).

Sex and Gender: in the 1970s second wave feminists along with sexologists argued that sex and gender are distinct from each other. They argued that gender is the result of social institutions and is a learned behaviour, where as sex is a biological category. Thus gender is a social construction and a product of nurturing, while sex is a fixed biological given and a product of nature. Feminist biologist Anne Fausto-Sterling recounts the history of the term in the following way:

> Feminists argued that although men's and women's bodies serve different reproductive functions, few other sex differences come with the territory, unchangeable by life's vicissitudes. If girls couldn't learn math as easily, the problem wasn't built into their brains. The difficulty resulted from gender norms – different expectations and opportunities for boys and girls. Having a penis, rather than a vagina is a sex difference. Boys performing better than girls on math exams is a gender difference. (2000: 4)

Traits like nurturing, connectedness, aggression, linear thinking, activity and passivity have been described as purely the result of gender. Physical attributes like breasts, vaginas, labia, oestrogen, testosterone, penises, testicles, semen and reproductive capacities have been labelled sex. Since the 1990s some thinkers have begun to problematise the sex/gender distinction. Tom Laqueur in *Making Sex* (1992) argues that prior to the late nineteenth century western thinking employed a one-sex model, a model that viewed women's reproductive organs as inverted, inferior forms of male reproductive organs. There were two genders, but one sex, according to Laqueur. **Elizabeth Grosz** in 'Experimental Desire: Rethinking Queer Subjectivity' (1994) argues that in thinking about sex and gender the theorist should not only focus on the instability of gender, but should 'focus on the instabilities of sex itself, of bodies themselves' (140). Thus both Grosz and Laqueur argue sex itself, like gender, is a social construction. Anne Fausto-Sterling in *Sexing the Body* (2000) argues that scientists create truths about sex and **sexuality** that become **embodied**. We come to see our bodies as sexed in the way that scientists construct our sex and sexuality. Furthermore, behaviours that we take to be gendered and purely social are connected to sexed bodies. These need to be understood together 'as part of a developmental system' (246). Thus Fausto-Sterling argues that we can see sex and gender as both being products of nurture and nature and must work to understand them together.

See **femininity; heteronormative**

Sexism: sexism is the institutional and individual **patriarchal oppression** of women that results from their sex as women and the tandem sex privileging given to men because they are men. In one of her earliest essays **Marilyn Frye** seeks to understand and define sexist. She says 'the term "sexist" in its core and perhaps most fundamental meaning is a term which characterizes anything whatever which creates, constitutes, promotes or exploits any irrelevant or impertinent marking of the distinction between the sexes' (referenced in 1983: 18).

In a later version of this essay, 'Sexism', in *Politics of Reality* (1983) Frye reworks this definition because she finds that she only focused on sexism as an individual act, not a structural or institutional oppression. She further argues that sex is not irrelevant in sexism because sex was relevant in the first place, i.e. there is a larger patriarchal structure predicated on the sex privilege of men, that allows sexism to take place. Frye's final, revised definition of sexist takes these considerations into account. She argues

> 'sexist' characterizes cultural and economic structures which create and enforce the elaborate and rigid patterns of sex-marking and sex-announcing which divide the species, along lines of sex, into dominators and subordinates. Individual acts and practices are sexist which reinforce and support those structures, either as culture or as shapes taken on by the enculturated animals. Resistance to sexism is that which undermines those structures by social and political action and by projects of reconstruction and revision of ourselves. (38)

It cannot be emphasised how much of feminist philosophy has been focused on the eradication of sexism; one could argue that it is one of the prime purposes of feminism. For example, **bell hooks** in her definition of feminism locates it as a movement to end sexism. She states '[f]eminism is the movement to end sexism, sexist exploitation, and oppression' (2000: viii).

Sexism is intimately tied to **racism, classism,** discrimination against people with disabilities, homophobia and numerous other oppressions.

Sexual division of labour: the sexual division of labour is when men and women perform different tasks in the home and in the workforce. For example, women in western societies do more childcare, cleaning and cooking in the home, whereas men are more likely to do tasks such as lawn mowing and taking out trash. In the workforce we see the sexual division of labour on all economic levels. For example, women are more likely to do home healthcare and men are more likely to do rubbish removal. Women are more likely to teach elementary/primary school and men are more likely to teach at the university level. In this dichotomy male jobs are usually viewed as more important and garner higher salaries. In the home, women's work usually goes unrecognised and is 'invisible labour'. Numerous feminists have critiqued the sexual division of labour, particularly **Marxist feminists** and **socialist feminists**. In her 2002 book, *Repair: The Impulse to Restore in a Fragile World*, **Elizabeth Spelman** analyses the gendered nature of repair through the sexual division of labour, from who repairs what, to the gendered norms of who is responsible for maintaining and fixing relationships.

Further reading: Jaggar (1988)

Sexual harassment: sexual harassment is an illegal form of gender discrimination and **oppression**. In the US it violates the Civil Rights Act of 1964 and in the UK it violates the newly amended (2005) Sexual Discrimination Act of 1975. Title VII of the US Civil Rights Act defines sexual harassment as follows:

Unwelcome sexual advances, requests for sexual favors, and other verbal or physical conduct of a sexual nature constitutes sexual harassment when submission to or rejection of this conduct explicitly or implicitly affects an individual's employment, unreasonably interferes with an individual's work performance or creates an intimidating, hostile or offensive work environment.

In the UK sexual harassment is legally defined as as follows:

A person subjects a woman to harassment, including sexual harassment, if: (a) on the ground of her sex, he engages in unwanted conduct that has the purpose or effect – (i) of violating her dignity, or (ii) of creating an intimidating, hostile, degrading, humiliating or offensive environment for her, (b) he engages in any form of unwanted verbal, non-verbal or physical conduct of a sexual nature that has the purpose or effect – (i) of violating her dignity, or (ii) of creating an intimidating, hostile, degrading, humiliating or offensive environment for her, or (c) on the ground of her rejection of or submission to unwanted conduct of a kind mentioned in paragraph (a) or (b), he treats her less favourably than he would treat her had she not rejected, or submitted to, the conduct.

Though most types of feminism have been concerned with sexual harassment, **liberal feminists** and **Marxist feminists** have written most explicitly about it.

Further reading: Hay (2005); Williams (2002); Zippel (2006)

Sexuality: sexuality is considered by many feminists to be a **social construction**; that is, it is a historical result of contextual historical events and constraints. This doesn't mean that sexuality is not linked to bodies, but it means that our way of thinking about sexual arrangements is a relatively recent historical phenomenon that comes out of our current preoccupations and concerns. Given this understanding of sexuality, sexuality is a set of 'social arrangements' that manifested in the late nineteenth, early twentieth centuries that include 'norms governing sex and reproduction – as cultural products amenable to change' (Nye, 1999: 5). Furthermore, sexuality includes desires and pleasures, who and how one can desire, habits, modes of interaction, ways of being, prohibitions and bodily practices. Sexuality has been important in many areas of feminist thought because it is part of the **patriarchal** social structure and is regulated by heteronormativity. For example, postmodern feminist **Luce Irigaray** opens up her essay 'Così Fan Tutti' (in Irigaray, 1985a) by arguing that 'psychoanalytic discourse on female sexuality is the discourse of truth. A discourse that tells the truth about the logic of truth: namely, that *the feminine occurs only within models and laws devised by male subjects*' (86). Furthermore, because of the **heternormative** nature of western culture, as Ladelle McWhorter argues in *Bodies and Pleasures* (1999), 'homosexuals are never judged by any criterion other than their sexuality, and the judgment is always negative' (3).

Shiva, Vandana: Shiva is an Indian physicist, **ecofeminist** and activist. She is one of the most active and well-known voices in the anti**globalisation** movement. Shiva argues for indigenous rights and environmental rights, focusing particularly on the theft of the intellectual commons and community resources by multinational corporations and other global organisations. Thus she argues against intellectual property rights that allow the patenting of indigenous knowledge by multinational corporations that resulted from the TRIPS Agreement (the World Trade Organisation's Trade-Related Aspects of Intellectual Property Rights), the privatisation and tariffing of water, genetically modified foods and the exploitation of women's labour. In her book *Biopiracy: The Plunder of Nature and Knowledge* (1997), she argues that globalisation, the contemporary mode of colonialism and imperialism, is leading to a lack of intellectual, agricultural and ecological diversity, resulting in an effective **monoculture**. Knowledge and life are 'pirated' by multinational corporations that then patent and market these as their own unique products to those in the North as well as back to people living in the South, leading to the epistemological and physical degradation of the Third World.

In *Water Wars: Privatization, Pollution, and Profit* (2002) Shiva argues that the commodification of water by exclusive irrigation, aquafarming, damming and mining by multinational corporations and national and state governments is leading to literal wars over water, the loss of cultural identity and the loss of means of living, as well as the erosion of democratic politics. Communal water not only represented important cultural commonality, it was a means of sustaining and creating life and livelihoods. Shrimp farming in India is a prime illustration of the complexity of the problems Shiva seeks to highlight. She states:

> Women have been particularly affected by the proliferation of the shrimp industry. Land has become a scarce commodity, and fights over patches of land are more and more frequent. Women in Pudukuppam, India must walk one to two kilometers to fetch drinking water. Wells have become sources of social tension. In the Indian village of Kuru, there is no drinking water available to the 600 residents due

to salinization. After the 1994 protests by the local women, water was supplied in tankers, with each household receiving only two pots per day for drinking, washing and cleaning. 'Our men need 10 buckets of water to bathe after their fishing trips. What can we do with two pots?' is what women of coastal villages said to me. In Andhra Pradesh, the government supplied water by tankers from a distance of 20 kilometers for two years before it finally decided to move the 500 families to another location. In a number of regions, relocation was not possible and residents had no option but to use saline water for their crops and everyday needs. (113)

Shiva uses this example to point to the displacement of communities, the loss of community resources, the loss of basic means of survival, and the tension and fighting in communities that result from the global demand for shrimp and multinational corporations' willingness to meet this demand (both of which are causes of and products of globalisation), despite the cost to affected communities.

Shiva's work has provided important insights for **feminist postcolonial theory, transnational feminism** and **anticapitalist feminism** as well as **ecofeminism**. Among her other books are *Stolen Harvest* (2000) and *Earth Democracy* (2005), and *Monocultures of the Mind* (1993), and she has co-edited *Ecofeminism* (1993).

Silvers, Anita: white US feminist philosopher specialising in social and political philosophy, disability studies, philosophy of law and bioethics. Silvers has made a number of contributions to feminist theory in most branches of philosophy, but her most recent contributions have been in **disability studies** and in bioethics. In *Disability, Difference, Discrimination: Perspectives on Justice in Bioethics and Policy* (1998), co-authored with David Wasserman and feminist bioethicist **Mary Mahowald**, Silvers' essay 'Formal Justice' argues for an environmental understanding of disability. An environmental understanding of disability is one in which we understand something to be a disability in light of what is lacking in one's environment. For example, in light of not having a ramp, not having the use of one's legs is a disability. In a community in which everything was easily accessible by wheelchair, not having the use of one's legs would not be a disability. Thus the goal would be to create a substantive change in the environment such that the environment is usable to all people. Silvers argues that in light of this understanding of disability, formal distributive justice in which goods are equitably distributed could be met by fully following the Americans with Disabilities Act 1990. Silvers is also the co-editor of *Medicine and Social Justice* (2002) and the co-author of *Puzzles About Art: An Aesthetics Casebook* (1989).

Situated Knowledge: situated knowledge has become a more general term for the idea that all knowledge originates from a particular perspective. Knowledge from any perspective is generated by the experiences one has in that location. **Donna Haraway** first uses this term in her article 'Situated Knowledge' in *Simians, Cyborgs and Women*. She argues that **standpoint epistemology** looks at perspective and location too narrowly and uncritically. According to Haraway all knowledge comes from a particular perspective; not only is this perspective a place from which to interrogate and know the world, but the location itself is also a place to be interrogated. In other words, one must be critical of the location from which she knows. Haraway does not see situated knowledge as a way to achieve objectivity, she thinks this is impossible, but she does think that a plurality of views, all coming from situated perspectives, will lead to more critical knowledge acquisition.

See **ecological thinking; feminist epistemology; feminist science studies; local knowledge**

Social Construction: to say that something is socially constructed means that it is the result of social norms, values and practices that organise what we know about or how we experience that thing, not the result of a deep **essential** nature. In other words, when something is socially constructed it is particular to that social, historical context and does not have a nature that endures in every context and is ahistorical. For example, to claim that **race** is a social construct means that even though race is socially attached to particular bodies, that is particular phenotypes, there is no biological basis for race. Instead race is 'a concept which signifies and symbolises social conflicts and interests by referring to different types of human bodies' (Omi and Winant, 1994: 55). Feminist theorists have argued that many things that we take to have essential natures are socially constructed; among these are **gender, sexuality,** beauty, knowledge (including scientific knowledge), race and sexual identity.

Smith, Barbara: African-American feminist theorist and activist. Barbara Smith is one of the founding members of the Combahee River Collective, a group of feminist African-American women who were 'actively committed to struggling against racial, sexual, heterosexual, and all oppression and see as our particular task the development of integrated analysis and practice based upon the fact that the major systems of oppression are interlocking'

(Combahee River Collective, 1981: 234). She also is one of the founders of the feminist Kitchen Table: A Woman of Color Press and the author of *The Truth That Never Hurts: Writings on Race, Gender, and Freedom* (2000). In the feminist movement Barbara Smith is well known for her incisive critiques of white culture and of the **oppression** faced by Black lesbians in both the white and the Black communities, by feminist and non-feminists. *The Truth That Never Hurts* is the first collection compiled by Smith that consists only of her own writings; she has edited numerous anthologies, such as *Home Girls: A Black Feminist Anthology* (2000), in which she includes her work with that of other feminists. In *The Truth That Never Hurts* Smith includes her well-known essay 'Toward a Black Feminist Criticism' in which she worked to make visible Black women writers, in particular Black lesbian writers and Black lesbian literary texts, and to argue for a distinctively Black feminist literary critical tradition. Smith argues that a 'Black feminist approach to literature that embodies the realization that the politics of sex as well as the politics of race and class are crucially interlocking factors in the works of Black women writers is an absolute necessity' (6).

See **Black feminist thought**

Socialist Feminism: socialist feminism 'is the development of a political theory and practice that will synthesise the best insights of radical feminism and of the Marxist tradition and that simultaneously will escape the problems associated with each' (Jaggar, 1988: 123). Furthermore, it 'seeks to explain the ways in which capitalism interacts with patriarchy to oppress women more egregiously than men' (Tong, 1998: 119). Unlike **liberal feminists** who believe that there is an adequate existing political structure that needs to be fully realised to end women's oppression, socialist feminists argue that new political and economic categories need to be generated in order to end **gender oppression**. Like other forms of feminism, they work to break down the distinction between the public and private spheres. They analyse the gendered nature of work, childcare, pregnancy and birth, and bodily practices such as weight management and grooming as products of historical construction not essential and/or biological. Unlike Marxist feminists they don't prioritise socialism over feminism. They see these projects as intimately intertwined. Socialist feminists see all forms of oppression as linked and the goal should be to end all oppression.

> Socialist feminists claim that a full understanding of the capitalist system requires a recognition of the way it is structured by male dominance and, conversely, that a full understanding of contemporary male dominance requires a recognition of the way it is organized by the capitalist division of labor. (Jaggar, 1988: 123)

They rethink the traditional Marxist reading of historical materialism (the historical development of economic relations, class antagonism and economic oppression) to understand its dialectical nature as an explanatory mode that not only explains **class** relations and economic oppression but the **sexual division of labour** and women's oppression in general, as well as other forms of oppression such as racial and sexual oppression.

Socialist feminism has not only social and political implications, but also epistemological implications. **Standpoint epistemology** developed from socialist feminist arguments. Some socialist feminists are **Alison Jaggar** and **Iris Young**.

See **Marxist feminism; radical feminism**

Society for Women in Philosophy: SWIP (Society for Women in Philosophy) was formed in 1971 by a group of US feminist philosophers 'to promote and support women in philosophy'. **Sandra Bartky** in the 'Introduction' to *Femininity and Domination* (1991) provides a brief history of the forming of SWIP. She states that it had its beginnings in the Women's Caucus of the American Philosophical Association and met for the first time in Chicago in 1971. In Bartky's words:

> There were a number of impulses behind the founding of SWIP, not the least of which was our desire to combine our professional identities as philosopher with our new-found identities as feminists. Most [of the early participants] had had few if any female colleagues in graduate school and no female teachers. Many had already spent years in profound professional isolation, dealing with academic sexism . . . We came together in joy and in solidarity. We talked all day and most of the night. We stared at one another and even touched each other, as if we were fabulous beasts. (2)

SWIP now has three US divisions, Eastern, Midwest and Pacific, and Canadian and British divisions. The feminist philosophy journal *Hypatia* was initiated by members of SWIP. SWIP continues to serve as a place for community, theorising and activism for feminist philosophers.

Spelman, Elizabeth: white US feminist philosopher specialising in social and political philosophy. Spelman is the author of the *Inessential Woman: Problems of Exclusion in Feminist Thought* (1990), one of the first book-length efforts by a white feminist to chart and critique feminist philosophy's exclusion of **Women of Colour** and issues of **race** and **class** from feminist theorising and practice.

In her 2002 book, *Repair: The Impulse to Restore in a Fragile World*, Spelman analyses the human impulse to repair. She works to understand the gendered nature of repair through the **sexual division of labour**, from who repairs what to the gendered norms of who is responsible for maintaining and fixing relationships.

Spivak, Gayatri Chakravorty: Indian feminist literary critic teaching in the US, specialising in postcolonial theory and deconstructionism. Spivak helped lay the groundwork for **postcolonial feminism** and **Third World feminism**. Her work came to the attention of the broader feminist community with her essay 'Can the Subaltern Speak?' (1988). In this essay she argues that the voice of the female **subaltern** is muted because academics have been trained to listen in the language of **hegemonic**, white, **androcentric**, **Eurocentric** discourse that is incapable of hearing the subaltern. Thus, when academics make claims about the subaltern, their work 'in the long run, cohere[s] with the work of imperialist subject-constitution, mingling epistemic violence with the advancement of learning and civilization. And the subaltern woman will be as mute as ever' (295). Thus, the subaltern woman is effectively silenced by the theorist that is claiming to speak for her. Spivak suggests that '[i]n seeking to learn to speak to (rather than listen to or speak for) the historically muted subject of the subaltern woman, the postcolonial intellectual *systematically* "unlearns" female privilege' (295). The intellectual has to learn to be critical of her own roles in **patriarchal** culture and postcolonial theory and unlearn her approach to her subject. This responsibility of 'unlearning' and learning to 'speak to' is a task the female intellectual 'must not disown with a flourish' (308).

Spivak also translated and provided an introduction to the first English edition of Derrida's *Of Grammatology* (1976) and is the author of *Outside In the Teaching*

Machine (1993), *A Critique of Post-Colonial Reason: Toward a History of the Vanishing Present* (1999) and *Death of a Discipline* (2003). In *Death of a Discipline* Spivak argues for a move from comparative literature that only considers literature to be a European pursuit to a broader comparison that includes the languages and peoples of the Southern hemisphere, the voice and the writing of the subaltern. For Spivak what is at stake is not just disciplinary, but ethical as well. Comparative literature must be reformed so that the languages and the peoples of the Southern Hemisphere are not treated merely as 'field languages' and objectified, but as 'active cultural media' that recognise the specificity of language and the privilege of literacy (9).

See **anti-racist feminism; decolonisation; transnational feminism**

Standpoint Epistemology: an insight borrowed from Hegel and Marx and adopted in various forms by some feminist thinkers, among them **Patricia Hill Collins Sandra Harding, Nancy Hartsock** and **Alison Jaggar**. Standpoint epistemologies hold that the view of oppressed groups is more critical than the view of those within dominant culture. It creates an overt connection between politics and knowledge. Standpoint epistemologists argue that **marginalised** groups have different perspectives of what and why something counts as truth, values, morality and justice. Because oppressed individuals and groups have less invested in being complicit in maintaining and participating in mainstream culture, they are more likely to provide a critical perspective. Thus the perspectives from oppressed lives are better locations from which to initiate critical knowledge-generating projects.

See **oppression; situated knowledge; socialist feminism**

Further reading: Collins (1990); Harding (1991); Hartsock (1999); Jaggar (1988)

Strategic Essentialism: a concept used first by **Gayatri Chakra-vorty Spivak** in her essays 'Can the Subaltern Speak?' (1988) and 'Subaltern Studies: Deconstructing Historiography' [1985] (1995) to indicate a political and temporary use of **essentialism** for the subversive ends of creating or understanding a group self-consciousness. Spivak, in her critique of the Subaltern Studies group, a working group of **postcolonial theorists**, argues that when she reads their work 'from within but against the grain' (1985: 214) she reads the project as an attempt to develop a narrow consciousness, a self-consciousness, that would allow the employment and deployment of a strategic essentialism to understand the **subaltern** woman. She says:

> I would suggest that elements in their text would warrant a reading of the project to retrieve the subaltern consciousness as the attempt to undo a massive historiographic metalepsis and 'situated' the effect of the subject as subaltern. I would read it, then, as a *strategic* use of positivist essentialism in a scrupulously visible political interest ... This would allow them to use the critical force of antihumanism, in other words, even as they share its constitutive paradox: that the essentializing moment, the object of their criticism, is irreducible. The strategy becomes most useful when 'consciousness' is being used in the narrow sense, as self-consciousness. (214)

Spivak makes clear that strategic essentialism is not a 'search for lost origins' (1988: 295) that locates a static historical subject, but a critical, temporary method of locating self-consciousness for strategic ends.

Luce Irigaray also develops a type of strategic essentialism in *This Sex Which Is Not One* (1985a). She uses the term mimicry or *mimétisme* to describe a type of oppositional discourse in which women assume the characteristics assigned to them by **phallocentric** culture in order to challenge phallocentrism and its description of and prescription for women. In Irigaray's words, *mimétisme* is

> [a]n interim strategy for dealing with the realm of discourse (where the subject is posited as masculine), in which the woman deliberately assumes the feminine style and posture assigned to her within this discourse in order to uncover the mechanisms by which it exploits her. (220)

An example of this would be women employing a feminine style of writing, *écriture féminine*, to argue against male stereotypes of women.

Strategic essentialism has been used in many areas of feminist philosophy, including but not limited to **postcolonial feminist theory, Chicana feminism and Latina feminism, feminist science studies** and **queer theory.**

Strong Objectivity: a term used by **Sandra Harding** in reaction to the 'weak' **objectivity** that she argues exists in mainstream scientific practice. Strong objectivity is both an ends and a means. It requires that scientists recognise themselves as historically, culturally and socially located subjects. An individual's and community's location informs and shapes their values, methodology, research agendas, research outcomes, interpretations of data and what they consider to be legitimate scientific pursuits; thus scientific knowledge is the result of **local knowledge.** Strong objectivity does not result from a value-free, neutral science. Some values help to create strong objectivity, such as 'fairness, honesty and detachment, which are moral and, indeed, [some] political values and interests' (1992: 579). Scientists also have to become open to new and rival opinions, willing to analyse and perhaps accept research results that do not accord with their own preconceived expectations and to understand and try alternative methodologies in order to maximise objectivity. Individuals and communities practise strong objectivity by engaging in what Harding calls strong or strategic reflexivity. Strong objectivity and **strong/strategic reflexivity** subject science to the same level of critique, responsibility and understanding to which we subject other social institutions and practices. Strong objectivity specifies strategies to recognise those cultural values that infuse, shape and legitimise current science by starting off from perspectives that have been typically undervalued in the sciences, especially those generated by postcolonial and feminist accounts. Harding argues that a standpoint epistemology that starts off from these postcolonial and feminist accounts is the best means to achieve strong objectivity.

Further reading: Harding (1991, 1998, 2006)

Strong/Strategic Reflexivity: a term utilised by **Sandra Harding** to designate a more critical version of **reflexivity**. Harding's 'strong' (1991) or 'strategic' (1998) reflexivity 'requires that the objects of inquiry be conceptualised as gazing back in all their cultural particularity' (1991: 163) and researchers be conceptualised as gazing back with their own acknowledged cultural particularity.

Strong/strategic reflexivity requires that the theorist recognise that their knowledge is infused with culture and is achieved through practising **strong objectivity**. Strong objectivity requires that scientists recognise themselves as subjects located in a historical, cultural and social matrix that informs and shapes their values, methodology, research agendas, research outcomes, interpretations of data and what is considered legitimate scientific pursuits. Strong objectivity specifies strategies to recognise those cultural values that infuse, shape and legitimise current science by starting off from perspectives that have been typically undervalued in the sciences, especially those generated by postcolonial and feminist accounts (Harding, 1998). Harding formulated strategic reflexivity partly as a reaction to what she calls weak notions of reflexivity originating from the strong programme in the sociology of science. She argues that the reflexivity generated by the strong programme has focused on the micropractices of science, thus analysing the practices internal to science, while ignoring the social practices (or macropractices) that are taken to be external to science. Weak reflexivity does not have a means for identifying the cultural factors that may influence what is taken to count as truth and knowledge. They, thus, cannot be reflexive in the more thorough and productive sense that Harding requires of reflexivity.

See **diffraction**

Subaltern: Gayatri Chakravorty Spivak asks the question 'Can the subaltern speak?' (283) in her important 1988 article 'Can the Subaltern Speak?' Her response to this question is 'the subaltern cannot speak' (308). The term subaltern refers to those oppressed, **marginalised** or colonised individuals and communities and was first used by Antonio Gramsci, an early twentieth-century Italian social theorist, to refer to oppressed economic classes. When Spivak claims that the subaltern cannot speak she is asserting that because academics (in her essay she is referring to postcolonial theorists) have been trained to listen in the language of **hegemonic**, white, **androcentric, Eurocentric** discourse they are incapable of hearing the subaltern. Thus when academics make claims about the subaltern, their work 'in the long run, cohere[s] with the work of imperialist subject-constitution, mingling epistemic

violence with the advancement of learning and civilization. And the subaltern woman will be as mute as ever'
(295). Thus the subaltern woman is effectively silenced
by the theorist that is claiming to speak for her. Spivak
suggests that '[i]n seeking to learn to speak to (rather
than listen to or speak for) the historically muted subject
of the subaltern woman, the postcolonial intellectual *systematically* "unlearns" female privilege' (295). Thus the
intellectual has to learn to be critical of her own roles in
patriarchal culture and postcolonial theory and unlearn
her approach to her subject. This task of 'unlearning' and
learning to 'speak to' is a responsibility the female intellectual 'must not disown with a flourish' (308). The 'subaltern' has become an important concept in **Third World
feminism** and **decolonisation**.

See **colonisation; decolonisation; oppression; other/
othering**

Symbolic: symbolic has several but interrelated meanings in
philosophy. In general it is a term used to designate the
part of language that makes signs and meanings. The symbolic makes it possible to point to something as something that has meaning. French psychoanalyst Jacques
Lacan argued that the symbolic is **phallocentric** and thus
women are excluded from the symbolic. French **postmodern feminist Luce Irigaray** argues that the symbolic order
is changeable and historically conditioned by power relations, not an inflexible, ahistorical system of signs. She
argrees with Lacan that the symbolic is phallocentric, but
doesn't think this results in a lack of language or meaning
for women. Instead, as the symbolic replicates the phallocentric order modelled on the unitary male penis, women
must create language based on their own sexuality. Irigaray argues that women's own feminine **sexuality** is plural, modelled on their own sexual organs, the labia that

are already two and maybe more, and their own orgasms as multiple. She states '[h]er sexuality is at least double, goes even further; it is plural' (1985a: 32). Just as the phallocentric order translates from sexuality through to language and theory, so does female sexuality. Feminine theory, language and social order will thus be multiple and pluralistic.

Julia Kristeva uses the term symbolic to denote 'the structure or grammar that governs the ways in which symbols can refer . . . and is the domain of position and judgement' (Kristeva and Oliver, 1997: xv). She describes the symbolic as one of two parts of language (the other is the **semiotic**). For Kristeva language becomes gendered not through the symbolic but through the semiotic. She argues that all biological constraints, including gender, are part of the semiotic. Because of this and language's dual dependency on the semiotic and symbolic, language reflects the embodiment (gender, genetics, family structures, etc.) that constitutes a person.

T

Third Wave Feminism: Heavily influenced by **postmodern feminism** and **Third World feminism** as well as strategically and critically employing the methodologies of a number of different types of feminism, third wave feminism embraces the contradictions that are generated by taking a pluralistic approach to the critical analysis of western culture, **oppression**, masculinity, **femininity**, **class, race** and **colonialism**. Leslie Heywood and Jennifer Drake in *Third Wave Agenda: Being Feminist, Doing Feminism* (1997) argue that what third wave feminists have learned from Third World feminism is to seek 'languages and images that account for multiplicity and difference, that negotiate contradiction in affirmative ways, and give voice to a politics of hybridity and coalition' (9). It challenges categories of **gender** and **sexuality**; is anti-**essentialist** or employs strategic essentialism – a mode of temporarily essentialising a diverse group of people with the goal of developing a common identity; is critical of **second wave feminism** as monolithic, white, middle-class and concerned with white middle-class concerns, and is critical of the what it sees as second wave's attempts to be like men. Even though third wave feminism is critical of some aspects of second wave feminism, third wave feminists tend to see themselves as in debt the strides made both politically and theoretically by second wave feminists.

Third wave feminists are concerned with a multiplicity of issues that affect women and other oppressed groups. For example, they provide critical analyses of **whiteness**, body image, media, sexuality, prostitution, job outsourcing, gender categories and cultural imperialism. An aspect of third wave feminism that is distinct from second and first wave feminism is that third wave feminism theorises about itself, considers how it is different from second wave feminism and seeks to understand its place in the twenty-first century. It is intentionally self-critical with several books that seek to explore what is third wave feminism. See, for example, Zack's *Inclusive Feminism: A Third Wave Theory of Women's Commonality* (2005), Henry's *Not My Mother's Sister: Generational Conflict and Third-Wave Feminism* (2004) and Gillis's *Third Wave Feminism: A Critical Exploration* (2004). It also uses contemporary media and pop culture to get its message across and to generate more feminist activism. See, for example, the Third Wave Foundation at http://www.thirdwavefoundation.org/. Some second wave feminists have been critical of third wave feminism arguing that it has lost the explicit focus on women and oppression and that it is not focused on activism. Third wave feminists respond that they are activist, though it may be in ways that are different from second wave feminism, and that they do take gender oppression seriously, but they do so within the context of attempting to understand it as a situated, shifting practice that is intimately tied to other forms of oppression and thus cannot be tackled separately.

Third World Feminism: the important anthology, *This Bridge Called My Back: Writings by Radical Women of Color,* edited by Cherríe Moraga and **Gloria Anzaldúa** (1981) is recognised by many as the first explicitly self-defining Third World feminist text. Third World feminism is a plurality of feminist approaches generated by Third World women/**women of colour**. Many Third World feminists use the terms 'Third World women' and 'women of colour' interchangeably. See, for example, **Chandra Talpade Mohanty** et al.'s *Third World Women and the Politics of Feminism* (1991) and Chela Sandoval's *Methodology of the Oppressed* (2000).

Mohanty, in her introduction to *Third World Women and the Politics of Feminism* (1991), describes Third World feminism as 'imagined communities of women with divergent histories and social locations, woven together by the *political* threads of opposition to forms of domination that are not only pervasive but also systematic' (4). She argues for the idea of an imagined community instead of a fixed, static community, or a biological or **essentialist** notion of community, because the daily lives of Third World women are so different, yet there are clear links between them that are united through political struggles. She says, '[t]he idea of imagined community is useful because it leads us away from essentialist notions of third world women struggles, suggesting political rather than biological or cultural bases for alliance' (4). Mohanty claims that what unites Third World feminists together is the means by which they theorise about the intersections of sexism, colonialism, imperialism, race, ethnicity, class, development, poverty, work and the corporatisation of culture and health while at the same time providing a critique of mainstream white feminism. Third World feminists see themselves as united in struggle even thought their specific concerns may be different.

Uma Narayan, in her 1997 book *Dislocating Cultures: Identities, Traditions, and Third-World Feminism*, provides a more narrow definition of Third World feminists as 'feminists who acquired feminist views and engaged in feminist politics in Third World countries (4). She does this as part of her methodology to address a larger issue, the distorted understandings of Third World feminism by both the First and the Third World.

See **anti-capitalist critique; anti-racist feminism; colonisation; decolonisation; transnational feminism**

Tong, Rosemarie: white US feminist philosopher specialising in bioethics. Tong has made many contributions to feminist theory, one of which is the authoring of a comprehensive book introducing feminist philosophy to students and new scholars in the area. Tong's *Feminist Thought: A More Comprehensive Introduction* (1998) covers virtually all of feminist philosophy, from ethical and social and political thought to epistemology, and provides coverage of feminist philosophy from a number perspectives including **Third World feminism, postmodern feminism** and **lesbian ethics**. Tong has also edited a number of anthologies on feminist philosophy, including *Feminist Philosophy: Essential Readings in Theory, Reinterpretation, and Application* (1994). Her book *Feminist Approaches to Bioethics* (1997) provides a comparative analysis of feminist and non-feminist approaches to bioethics and shows how feminist approaches to reproductive technology differ from non-feminist approaches. Tong claims that feminist bioethics

> have almost always faulted the dominant nonfeminist approaches to bioethics for emphasizing rules over relationships, norms over virtues, and justice over caring. [But] provided that the principles of autonomy, beneficence, and justice address gender-related issues in historical context, feminist bioethicists find these principles useful. (3)

Tong argues that all feminist bioethics share a methodology that asks questions from the perspective of women, seek to raise consciousness about the **oppression** of women, and work to bridge the gap between theory and practice.

Transgenderist: transgenderist is a term that has supplanted the term transsexual to indicate new **gender** options in addition to sexual reassignment surgery. Transgender theorist Ann Bolin states in her article 'Transcending and Transgendering' that '[*t*]ransgenderist is a community term denoting kinship among those with gender-variant identities. It supplants the dichotomy of transsexual and transvestite with a concept of continuity' (1993: 461). Kate Bornstein, transgender activist and writer, makes clear the complexity of the transgender experience in her book *Gender Outlaw: On Men, Women and the Rest of Us* (1995). Bornstein states:

> I know I'm not a man – about that much I'm very clear, and I've come to the conclusion that I'm probably not a woman either, at least according to a lot of people's rules on this sort of thing. The trouble is we're living in a world that insists that we be one or the other – a world that doesn't bother to tell us exactly what one of the other *is*. (8)

See **heteronormative**
Further reading: Fausto-Sterling (2000); Herdt (1993)

Transnational Feminism: transnational feminism emerged from **postcolonial feminism** and **Third-World feminism** and is part of **decolonisation**. Inderpal Grewal and Caren Kaplan in their book *Scattered Hegemonies: Postmodernity and Transnational Feminism* (1994) state that the term transnational feminism is used as a way to distinguish between global feminism and international feminism because those terms and perspectives don't help in theorising about how borders, nations and categories change. They state that '[t]ransnational feminist practices refer us to the interdisciplinary study of the relationships between women in diverse parts of the world. These relationships are uneven, often unequal, and complex. They emerge from women's diverse needs and agendas in many cultures and societies' (2). **Chandra Talpade Mohanty** and Jacqui Alexander in *Feminist Genealogies, Colonial Legacies, Democratic Futures* (1996) argue that transnational feminism is not a theoretical position that merely 'fills in the gaps' in western feminism, nor does it attempt to work under the ideological weight of western feminism. 'Instead, it provides a position from which to argue for a comparative, relational feminist praxis that is transnational in its response to and engagement with global processes of colonization' (xx). Transnational feminism in not 'global sisterhood (defined as a "center/periphery" or "first-world/Third-World" model)' (xxix).

See anti-capitalist critique; anti-racist feminism

Tuana, Nancy: white US feminist philosopher specialising in feminist science studies and feminist epistemology. In *The Less Noble Sex* (1993) Nancy Tuana traces the historical undervaluing, **oppression** and assumed inferiority of women. She analyses the ways in which scientific, religious and philosophical views of women were generated that reflected women's status as inferior – biologically, intellectually and morally – while at the same time reinforcing women's status as inferior. Tuana analyses both biblical creation stories, historical anatomy texts and philosophical writings to provide her critical analysis. Tuana's anthology *Feminism and Science* published in 1989 is one of the first anthologies on feminist science studies. This reader paved the way for creating increased interest among feminist philosophers for the interdisciplinary work that is done in feminist science studies. Her other books include *Women and the History of Philosophy* (1992), and two edited volumes, *Revealing Male Bodies* (2001a) and *enGendering Rationalities* (2001b).

U

Universal: to say that a claim or a value is universal means that it can be applied consistently everywhere, at all times. Thus a universal claim would apply just as much in New Jersey as it does in Guatemala City. Furthermore, it would have applied in the eighteenth and the twenty-first centuries. Some feminists support the idea of universal claims. For example, In her book *Women and Human Development: The Capabilities Approach* (2001) **Martha Nussbaum** employs a type of universalism, arguing that it is the job of liberal democracy to provide its citizens with opportunities to realise their capabilities – what people are capable of doing or becoming – so that all people's needs are met at the minimum threshold required for the development of the whole community. Nussbaum formulates a capabilities approach that is attentive to different needs and capacities while being at the same time universalist. Nussbaum applies her capabilities approach to the situation of poor and marginally poor women in India, though she argues that it is applicable to the situation of all women.

Alice Walker describes **womanist** as universalist. She tells us that it is '[t]raditionally universalist, as in: "Mama, why are we brown, pink, and yellow, and our cousins are white, beige, and black?" Ans.: "Well, you know the colored race is just like a flower garden, with every color flower represented" ' (1983: xi). According to Walker, all people are people of colour. The universalisation of colour survives to unite seemingly disparate groups.

Some feminists have argued that universal claims are frequently generated by the dominant group and benefit that group's values. Thus particular claims that are taken to be universal are frequently harmful to marginalised groups because they were never meant to benefit them. For example, some feminists may argue that a universal assertion of the right to free speech allows hate speech to exist unregulated and appear not to be substantively different than other speech acts (Matsuda and Charles, 1993).

See **essentialism**; **objectivity**; **rationality**; **social construction**

W

Warren, Karen: white US feminist specialising in **ecofeminism**. Warren is the author of *Ecofeminist Philosophy: A Western Perspective on What It Is and Why It Matters* (2000) as well as numerous other ecofeminist texts. Warren argues that '[e]cological feminists ("ecofeminists") claim that there are important connections between the unjustified dominations of women, people of colour, children, and the poor and the unjustified domination of nature' (1). Warren points to many connections between the domination of women and nature that have been cited by ecofeminists. For example, she points to prevailing **dualisms** in western philosophy as a source of conceptual and practical domination. Man/woman, culture/nature, mind/body, reason/emotion exist as hierarchical dualisms in western thought with man, culture, mind and reason having higher value than women, nature, body and emotion. This conceptual dualism leads to the practical outcome of the valued half of the dualism having 'power over' the devalued half and thus the 'twin' domination of women and nature (Warren, 2000). The power of these dualisms transfers to language so that language is sexist-naturist. Warren points to sexist-naturist language that describes women as 'bitches' or 'fresh meat' and Native Americans as 'primitive' and 'uncultivated' as a 'language of domination' (60). She seeks to 'quilt' ecofeminism with ecology, feminism, science and technology development and argues that ecofeminism is essential to feminist philosophy to provide insights about 'women-other human-Others interconnections' (2000: 43). Furthermore, Warren holds that solutions to **gender oppression** and environmental problems should also include ecofeminist perspectives.
    See **Plumwood, Val**

Whiteness: though 'white' refers to people of European decent, feminists are concerned about whiteness because of what some refer to as 'white skin privilege'. In other words, white gets one things that a person of colour is not privileged to get and is actively prevented from getting. In her essay 'On Being White' (in Frye, 1984) white US feminist **Marilyn Frye** describes the epistemic and social benefits accorded to whites. According to Frye, whiteness allows whites to choose to listen and to hear, to choose who counts as white, to generate universals, to claim that 'others' are just like whites, to ignore and to be ignorant. Frye writes about the power of the ability to ignore that is conferred by whiteness. She says:

> Ignorance is not something simple: it is not a simple lack, absence, or emptiness, and it is not a passive state. Ignorance of this sort – the determined ignorance most white Americans have of American Indian tribes and clans, the ostrichlike ignorance most white Americans have of Black language – ignorances of these sorts is a complex result of many acts and many negligences. (118)

Frye argues that white is a 'political category' and though one can't change one's skin colour, one can resist whiteness by giving oneself the command to stop being white, by working not to benefit from white skin privilege through 'assuming responsibility' and by using 'radical imagination' (127).

See **epistemology of ignorance**

Womanist: a term first used by novelist, essayist and poet Alice Walker in *In Search of Our Mother's Gardens: Womanist Prose* (1983). Walker describes the term as originating from the African-American folk term 'womanish', meaning acting like a woman. Walker describes a womanist as a 'black feminist or a feminist of color' (1983, xi). She chooses the word womanist because it describes '. . . women who love other women, yes, but women who also have concern, in a culture that oppresses all black people (and this would go back very far), for their fathers, brothers, and sons, no matter how they feel about them as males.' Womanist has a spiritual and practical sense to it as well as being theoretical and applied. It is a word that does not divide women from women or is separatist. Walker sees the term as 'consistent with black cultural values' by 'affirm[ing] connectedness to the entire community and the world, rather than separation, *regardless* of who worked and slept with whom' (1983, 81). Thus Walker's term is universalist. She tells us that it is '[t]raditionally universalist, as in: "Mama, why are we brown, pink, and yellow, and our cousins are white, beige, and black?" Ans.: "Well, you know the colored race is just like a flower garden, with every color flower represented" (1983: xi). According to Walker, all people are people of colour. The universalisation of colour survives to unite seemingly disparate groups.

In terms of womanist's relationship to feminism, Walker tells her readers that '[w]omanist is to feminist as purple is to lavender' (xii). In other words, feminism is a type of womanism. Some other womanist thinkers are Katie Canon, Toni Morrison and Gloria Naylor.

See **Black feminist thought; universal; women of colour**

Women of Colour: women of colour and Third World women are frequently used interchangeably. The term came into prominent academic usage with Cherríe Moraga and **Gloria Anzaldúa's** *This Bridge Called My Back: Writings By Radical Women of Color* (1981), which was the first anthology to bring together the writings of a diverse group of feminist writers who self-consciously thought of themselves as women of colour. These writers were responding to the imperialism and **whiteness** of US culture as well as the whiteness of mainstream feminism, while at the same time forging their own theoretical perspectives as outsiders. Thus their project, and the term women of colour, is not just reactionary, it is an activist project forging unique, important and critical theories based on the lived experience of women of colour. **Chandra Talpade Mohanty** (2003) argues that what unites women into the category 'women of colour' is not race, ethnicity or skin colour, but is instead that they share a context for struggle that results from experiences of **racism** and imperialism. *This Bridge Called My Back: Writings By Radical Women of Color* described the areas of concerns and activism for women of colour in the following way:

1) how visibility/invisibility as Women of Color forms our radicalism; 2) the ways in which Third World women derive a feminist political theory specifically from our racial/cultural background and experience; 3) the destructive and demoralizing effects of racism in the women's movement; 4) the cultural, class, and sexuality differences that divide Women of Color; 5) Third World women's writing as a tool for self-preservation and evolution; and 6) the ways and means of a Third World feminist future. (Moraga and Anzaldúa, 1981: liii)

See **Third World feminism**; **transnational feminism**

Y

Young, Iris Marion: white US feminist philosopher specialising in ethics, social and political philosophy, and Continental philosophy. Young's work in social and political philosophy has centred on questions of justice and democratic theory. In her book *Justice and the Politics of Difference* (1990) Young positions herself against John Rawls's distributive justice arguing that it cannot adequately account for and address the problems of domination and **oppression**. She provides the 'five faces of oppression', which consist of **marginalisation**, exploitation, powerlessness, cultural imperialism and violence, as a framework through which to understand oppression. Her 2002 book, *Inclusion and Democracy* (2002), works from the perspective of critical theory, a mode of social analysis initiated by the Frankfurt School in the 1930s that initiates arguments from a historically and materially situated perspective. Young develops arguments for an inclusive understanding of democracy generated from the plurality of different ways that people communicate. Included in these are everyday communications and interactions, the tone of discourse, figures of speech, placards, narrative, and a responsiveness to social differences and to community needs and actions. Among Young's other work in political theory is *Intersecting Voices* (1997).

Young has also been an important figure in the study of female embodiment. Her essay 'Throwing Like a Girl' (1980) was one of the first essays on embodiment from a feminist perspective. In this essay she argues that **hegemonic** norms of femininity are used to keep women from reaching their full potential. Women learn to conceive of their bodies as soft, passive and unathletic, and learn to comport themselves and carry their bodies to mimic this cultural norm. Her work on embodiment has been collected in a volume entitled *On Female Body Experience: 'Throwing Like a Girl' and Other Essays* (2005).

Z

Zack, Naomi: Jewish, African-American and Native American feminist philosopher specialising in race theory, philosophy of science and modern philosophy. In her book *Race and Mixed Race* (1994) Zack challenges racial categories, arguing that the racial categories Black and white, as well as mixed **race** categories, reify and reinscribe **racism** because these categories, themselves, are products of the racist belief in pure races. In her 2005 book *Inclusive Feminism: A Third Wave Theory of Women's Commonality* (2005) Zack points to the problems that resulted from intersectionality in feminism, which was a reaction to the fragmentation in feminist theory that resulted from the false universalisation of white middle-class feminist women's experience in **second wave feminism**. Zack argues for an FMP (female from birth, biological mothers, or primary sexual choice of men) as a commonality, what she calls a relational **essentialism**, to unite all women. Through this commonality women can form political groups with substantial enough voting power to have a chance to win elections or change the ideological structure of current political parties. Among Zack's other books are *Bachelors of Science: Seventeenth-Century Identity, Then and Now* (1996) and *Philosophy of Race and Science* (2002).

Bibliography

Addelson, Kathryn Pyne (1992) *Impure Thoughts: Essays on Philosophy, Feminism, Ethics*. Philadelphia: Temple University Press.

Addelson, Kathryn Pyne (1994) *Moral Passages: Toward a Collectivist Moral Theory*. New York: Routledge.

Alcoff, Linda Martín (1996) *Real Knowing: A New Version of Coherence Theory*. Ithaca, NY: Cornell University Press.

Alcoff, Linda Martín (2006) *Visible Identities: Race, Gender, and the Self*. New York: Oxford University Press.

Alcoff, Linda Martín and Mendieta, Eduardo (eds) (2002) *Identities: Race, Class, Gender and Nationality*. New York: Blackwell.

Alcoff, Linda Martín and Potter, Elizabeth (eds) (1993) *Feminist Epistemologies*. New York: Routledge.

Anzaldúa, Gloria (ed.) (1990) *Making Face, Making Soul/Haciendo Caras: Creative and Critical Perspectives by Feminists of Color*. San Francisco: Aunt Lute Books.

Anzaldúa, Gloria [1987] (1999) *Borderlands/La Frontera*, 2nd edn. San Francisco: Aunt Lute Books.

Anzaldúa, Gloria and Keating, AnaLouise (2000) *Interviews/Entrevistas*. New York: Routledge.

Anzaldúa, Gloria and Keating, AnaLouise (ed.) (2002) *This Bridge We Call Home: Radical Visions for Transformation*. New York: Routledge.

Atherton, Margaret (ed.) (1994) *Women Philosophers of the Early Modern Period*. New York: Hackett.

Banks, Olive (1987) *Becoming a Feminist: The Social Origins of 'First Wave' Feminism*. Atlanta, GA: University of Georgia Press.

Barrett, Michèle (1989) *Women's Oppression Today: The Marxist/Feminist Encounter*. London: Verso Press.

Barrett, Michèle (1991) *The Politics of Truth: From Marx to Foucault*. Cambridge: Polity Press.

Barrett, Michèle (1999) *Imagination in Theory: Culture, Writing, Words, and Things*. New York: New York University Press.

Barrett, Michèle and McIntosh, Mary (1991) *The Anti-Social Family*. London: Verso Press.

Bartky, Sandra (1991) *Femininity and Domination: Studies in the Phenomenology of Oppression*. New York: Routledge.

Bartky, Sandra (2002) *Sympathy and Solidarity: and Other Essays*. New York: Rowman & Littlefield.

Beauvoir, Simone de (1967) *The Ethics of Ambiguity*. New York: Citadel Press.

Beauvoir, Simone de (1999) *America Day By Day*. Berkeley, CA: University of California Press.

Beauvoir, Simone de [1952] (1974) *The Second Sex*, trans. and ed. H. M. Parsley. New York: Vintage Books.

Benhabib, Seyla (1992) *Situating the Self*. New York: Routledge.

Benhabib, Seyla (1996a) *Democracy and Difference*. Princeton, NJ: Princeton University Press.

Benhabib, Seyla (1996b) *The Reluctant Modernism of Hannah Arendt*. New York: Rowman & Littlefield.

Benhabib, Seyla (2002) *The Claims of Culture*. Princeton, NJ: Princeton University Press.

Benhabib, Seyla (2004) *The Rights of Others*. Cambridge: Cambridge University Press.

Bolin, Anne (1993) 'Transcending and Transgendering: Male to Female Transexuals, Dichotomy and Diversity', in Gilbert Herdt (ed.), *Third Sex, Third Gender: Beyond Sexual Dimorphism in Culture and in History*. New York: Zone Books.

Bordo, Susan (1987) *The Flight to Objectivity*. New York: SUNY Press.

Bordo, Susan (1993) *Unbearable Weight*. Berkeley, CA: University of California Press.

Bordo, Susan (1999) *Twilight Zones*. Berkeley, CA: University of California Press.

Bordo, Susan (2000) *Male Bodies*. New York: Farrar, Straus & Giroux.

Bornstein, Kate (1995) *Gender Outlaw: On Men, Women and the Rest of Us*. New York: Vintage.

Braidotti, Rosi (1991) *Patterns of Dissonance*. New York: Routledge.

Braidotti, Rosi (1994) *Nomadic Subjects*. New York: Columbia University Press.

Braidotti, Rosi (2002) *Metamorphoses: Toward a Materialist Theory of Becoming*. Cambridge: Polity Press

Brand, Peggy Zeglin and Korsmeyer, Carolyn (ed.) (1995) *Feminism and Tradition in Aesthetics*. State College, PA: Pennsylvania State University Press.

Brooks, Ann (1997) *Postfeminisms*. London: Routledge.

Butler, Judith (1990) *Gender Trouble: Feminism and the Subversion of Identity*. New York: Routledge.

Butler, Judith (1993) *Bodies that Matter*. New York: Routledge.

Butler, Judith (2004) *Undoing Gender*. New York: Taylor & Francis.

Card, Claudia (ed.) (1991) *Feminist Ethics*, Lawrence, KS: University Press of Kansas.

Card, Claudia (1995) *Lesbian Choices*. New York: Columbia University Press.

Card, Claudia (2005) *The Atrocity Paradigm*. New York: Oxford University Press.

Cixous, Hélène (1983) 'Laugh of Medusa', in Elizabeth Abel and Emily K. Abel (eds), *The Signs Reader: Women, Gender, and Scholarship*. Chicago: University of Chicago Press.

Cixous, Hélène (1991) *'Coming to Writing' and Other Essays*. Cambridge, MA: Harvard University Press.

Cixous, Hélène [1986] (1999) 'Sorties', in J. Kourany et al. (eds), *Feminist Philosophies*. Saddle River, NJ: Prentice Hall, pp. 440–5.

Code, Lorraine (1981) 'Is the Sex of the Knower Epistemologically Significant?', *Metaphilosophy*, 12: 267–76.

Code, Lorraine (1987) *Epistemic Responsibility*. New Haven, CT: University Press of New England.

Code, Lorraine (1991) *What Can She Know? Feminist Theory and the Construction of Knowledge*. Ithaca, NY: Cornell University Press.

Code, Lorraine (1995) *Rhetorical Spaces: Essays on Gendered Locations*. New York: Routledge.

Code, Lorraine (2006) *Ecological Thinking: The Politics of Epistemic Location*. New York: Oxford University Press.

Collins, Patricia Hill (1986) 'Learning from the Outsider Within: The Sociological Significance of Black Feminist Thought', *Social Problems*, 33 (6): 14–32.

Collins, Patricia Hill (1991) *Black Feminist Thought: Knowledge, Consciousness and the Politics of Empowerment*. New York: Routledge.

Collins, Patricia Hill (1998) *Fighting Words: Black Women and the Search for Justice*. Minneapolis, MN: University of Minnesota Press.

Collins, Patricia Hill (2005) *Black Sexual Politics: African Americans, Gender, and the New Racism*. New York: Routledge.

Collins, Patricia Hill (2006) *From Black Power to Hip Hop: Racism, Nationalism, and Feminism*. Philadelphia: Temple University Press.

Combahee River Collective (1981) 'A Black Feminist Statement', in Cherríe Moraga and Gloria Anzaldúa (eds), *This Bridge Called My Back*. Berkeley, CA: 3rd Woman Press.

Cudd, Ann E. (2005) 'Missionary Positions', *Hypatia*, 20 (4): 164–82.

Daly, Mary (1968) *The Church and the Second Sex*. Boston: Beacon Press.

Daly, Mary (1973) *Beyond God the Father: Toward a Philosophy of Women's Liberation*. Boston: Beacon Press.

Daly, Mary (1978) *Gyn/Ecology: The Metaethics of Radical Feminism*. Boston: Beacon Press.

Daly, Mary (1984) *Pure Lust: Elemental Feminist Philosophy*. New York: Women's Press.

Daly, Mary (1992) *Outercourse: Be Dazzling Voyage*. San Francisco: Harper.

Daly, Mary (1999) *Quintessence ... Realizing the Archaic Future*. Boston: Beacon Press.

Derrida, Jacques (1976) *Of Grammatology*, trans. Gayatri Chakravorty Spivak. Baltimore, MD: Johns Hopkins University Press.

Deutscher, Max (ed.) (2001) *Michèle Le Dœuff: Operative Philosophy and Imaginary Practice*. New York: Humanity Books.

Eisenstein, Zillah (2001) *Manmade Breast Cancers*. Ithaca, NY: Cornell University Press.

Engels, Friedrich (1884/1972) *The Origin of the Family*. New York: International Publishers.

Fausto-Sterling, Anne (2000) *Sexing the Body*. New York: Basic Books.

Firestone, Shulamith (1970) *The Dialectic of Sex*. New York: Farrar, Straus & Giroux.

Foucault, Michel (1990) *The History of Sexuality*. New York: Vintage.

Fraser, Nancy (1996) *Justice Interruptus: Critical Reflections on the 'Postsocialist' Condition*. New York: Routledge.

Fraser, Nancy and Honnet, Axel (2003) *Redistribution or Recognition? A Political-Philosophical Exchange*. New York: Verso.

Friedan, Betty [1963] (2001) *The Feminine Mystique*. New York: W. W. Norton.

Frye, Marilyn (1983) *The Politics of Reality*. Freedom, CA: Crossing Press.

Frye, Marilyn (1991) 'A Response to *Lesbian Ethics*: Why *Ethics*?', in Claudia Card (ed.), *Feminist Ethics*. Lawrence, KS: University of Kansas Press.

Frye, Marilyn (1992) *The Willful Virgin*. Freedom, CA: Crossing Press.

Gatens, Moira (1991) *Feminism and Philosophy: Perspectives on Difference and Equality*. Bloomington, IN: Indiana University Press.

Gatens, Moira (1995) *Imaginary Bodies: Ethics, Power, Corporeality*. New York: Routledge.

Gatens, Moira and Lloyd, Genevieve (1999b) *Collective Imaginings: Spinoza, Past and Present*. New York: Routledge.

Gatens, Moira et al. (eds) (1999a) *Australian Feminism: A Companion*. Oxford: Oxford University Press.

Gilligan, Carol (1982) *In a Different Voice*. Cambridge, MA: Harvard University Press.

Gilligan, Carol (1991) *Women, Girls, and Psychotherapy: Reframing Resistance*. Chicago: Harrington Press.

Gilligan, Carol (2003) *The Birth of Pleasure*. New York: Vintage.

Gillis, Stacy (2004) *Third Wave Feminism: A Critical Exploration*. New York: Palgrave Macmillan.

Grewal, Inderpal and Kaplan, Caren (1994) *Scattered Hegemonies: Postmodernity and Transnational Feminism*. Minneapolis, MN: University of Minnesota Press.

Grosz, Elizabeth (1994a) 'Experimental Desire: Rethinking Queer Subjectivity', in J. Copjec (ed.), *Supposing the Subject*. New York: Verso, pp. 133–56.

Grosz, Elizabeth (1994b) *Volatile Bodies*. Bloomington, IN: Indiana University Press.

Grosz, Elizabeth (2001) *Architecture from the Outside: Essays on Virtual and Real Space*. Boston: MIT Press.

Grosz, Elizabeth (2005a) *Nick of Time: Politics, Evolution, and the Untimely*. Durham, NC: Duke University Press.

Grosz, Elizabeth (2005b) *Time Travels: Feminism, Nature, Power*. Durham, NC: Duke University Press.

Haraway, Donna (1989) *Primate Visions*. New York: Routledge.

Haraway, Donna (1991) *Simians, Cyborgs and Women*. New York: Routledge.

Haraway, Donna (1997) *Modest Witness at Second Millennium*. New York: Routledge.

Harding, Sandra (1986) *The Science Question in Feminism*. Ithaca, NY: Cornell University Press.

Harding, Sandra (1991) *Whose Science? Whose Knowledge?* Ithaca, NY: Cornell University Press.

Harding, Sandra (ed.) (1993) *The 'Racial' Economy of Science: Toward a Democratic Future*. Bloomington, IN: Indiana University Press.

Harding, Sandra (1998) *Is Science Multicultural?* Bloomington, IN: Indiana University Press.

Hartsock, Nancy (1985) *Money, Sex and Power: Toward a Feminist Historical Materialism*. Boston: Northeastern University Press.

Hartsock, Nancy (1999) *The Feminist Standpoint Revisited and Other Essays*. Boulder, CO: Westview Press.

Hay, Carol (2005) 'Whether to Ignore Them and Spin: Moral Obligations of Resist Sexual Harassment', *Hypatia*, 20 (4): 94–108.

Held, Virginia (1989) *Rights and Goods: Justifying Social Action*. Chicago: University of Chicago Press.

Held, Virginia (1993) *Feminist Morality: Transforming Culture, Society, and Politics*. Chicago: University of Chicago Press.

Held, Virginia (2002) 'Care and the Extension of Markets', *Hypatia*, 17 (2): 19–33.

Held, Virginia (2005) *The Ethics of Care: Personal, Political, and Global*. New York: Oxford University Press.

Henry, Astrid (2004) *Not My Mother's Sister: Generational Conflict and Third-Wave Feminism*. Bloomington, IN: Indiana University Press.

Herdt, Gilbert (ed.) (1993) *Third Sex, Third Gender: Beyond Sexual Dimorphism in Culture and in History*. New York: Zone Books.

Heywood, Leslie and Drake, Jennifer (eds) (1997) *Third Wave Agenda: Being Feminist, Doing Feminism*. Minneapolis, MN: University of Minnesota Press.

Hoagland, Sarah (1989) *Lesbian Ethics*. Amherst, MA: Institute for Lesbian Studies.

Hoagland, Sarah (1994) 'Lesbian Ethics', in Mary Mahowald (ed.), *Philosophy of Women*. New York: Hackett, pp. 451–64.

hooks, bell (1981) *Ain't I a Woman? Black Women and Feminism*. Boston: South End Press.

hooks, bell (1984) *Feminist Theory: From Margin to Centre*. Boston: South End Press.

hooks, bell (1992) *Black Looks: Race and Representation*. Boston: South End Press.

hooks, bell (1994) *Teaching to Transgress*. New York: Routledge.

hooks, bell (2000) *Feminism Is for Everybody: Passionate Politics*. Boston: South End Press.

hooks, bell (2001) *All About Love: New Visions*. New York: William Morrow.

hooks, bell (2004) *The Will to Change: Men, Masculinity, and Love*. New York: Atria Books.

Irigaray, Luce (1985b) *The Speculum of the Other Woman*. Ithaca, NY: Cornell University Press.

Irigaray, Luce, (1985a) *This Sex Which Is Not One*. Ithaca, NY: Cornell University Press.

Jaggar, Alison (1988) *Feminist Politics and Human Nature*. New York: Rowman & Littlefield.

Jagose, Annamarie (1997) *Queer Theory: An Introduction*. New York: New York University Press.

Keating, AnaLouise (ed.) (2005) *EntreMundos/AmongWorlds: New Perspectives on Gloria Anzaldúa*. New York: Palgrave Macmillan.

Kittay, Eva (1987) *Metaphor: Its Cognitive Force and Linguistic Structure*. Oxford: Oxford University Press.

Kittay, Eva (1999) *Love's Labor: Essays on Women, Equality, and Dependency*. New York: Routledge.

Kittay, Eva and Feder, Ellen (2002) *Theoretical Perspectives on Dependency and Women*. New York: Rowman & Littlefield.

Knudsen, Lara M. and Hartmann, Hartmann (2006) *Reproductive Rights in a Global Context: South Africa, Uganda, Peru, Denmark, the United States, Vietnam, Jordan*. Nashville, TN: Vanderbilt University Press.

Korsmeyer, Caroline (2004) *Gender and Aesthetics*. New York: Routledge.

Kristeva, Julia (1980) *The Powers of Horror*. New York: Columbia University Press.

Kristeva, Julia with Oliver, Kelly (ed.) (1997) *The Portable Kristeva*. New York: Columbia University Press.

Lacan, Jacques (1981) *The Language of the Self: The Function of Language in Psychoanalysis*, trans. Anthony Wilden. Baltimore, MD: Johns Hopkins University Press.

Laqueur, Thomas Walter (1992) *Making Sex: Body and Gender from the Greeks to Freud*. Cambridge, MA: Harvard University Press.

Le Dœuff, Michèle (2000) 'Feminism Is Back in France – Or Is It?', *Hypatia*, 15 (4): 243–55.

Le Dœuff, Michèle (2003a) *The Sex of Knowing*, trans. Kathryn Hamer and Lorraine Code. New York: Routledge.

Le Dœuff, Michèle (2003b) *The Philosophical Imaginary*. New York: Continuum International.

Lindemann, Hilde (2005) *An Invitation to Feminist Ethics*. New York: McGraw-Hill.

Lloyd, Genevieve (1984) *The Man of Reason: 'Male' and 'Female' in Western Philosophy*. New York: Routledge.

Lloyd, Genevieve (ed.) (2002) *Feminism and the History of Philosophy*. Oxford: Oxford University Press.

Lloyd, Genevieve and Gatens, Moira (1999) *Collective Imaginings: Spinoza, Past and Present*. New York: Routledge.

Longino, Helen (1990) *Science as Social Knowledge*. Princeton, NJ: Princeton University Press.

Longino, Helen (2002) *The Fate of Knowledge*. Princeton, NJ: Princeton University Press.

Lorde, Audre (1980) *The Cancer Journals*. Boston: Aunt Lute Books.

Lorde, Audre (1983) *Zami: A New Spelling of My Name*. Freedom, CA: Crossing Press.

Lorde, Audre (1984) *Sister Outsider*. Freedom, CA: Crossing Press.

Lorde, Audre (1990) 'I Am Your Sister: Black Women Organizing Across Sexualities', in Gloria Anzaldúa (ed.), *Making Face, Making Soul/Haciendo Caras: Creative and Critical Perspectives by Feminists of Color*. San Francisco: Aunt Lute Books.

Lorde, Audre (1995) *The Black Unicorn*. New York: W. W. Norton.

Lugones, María (1987) 'Playfulness, "World"-traveling, and Loving Perception', *Hypatia*, 2 (2): 3–20.

Lugones, María (1990) 'Hablando cara a cara/Speaking Face to Face: An Exploration of Ethnocentric Racism', in Gloria Anzaldúa (ed.), *Making Face, Making Soul/Haciendo Caras: Creative and Critical Perspectives by Feminists of Color*. San Francisco: Aunt Lute Books.

Lugones, María (1991) 'On the Logic of Pluralist Feminism', in Claudia Card (ed.), *Feminist Ethics*. Lawrence, KS: University of Kansas Press.

Lugones, María (2003) *Pilgrimages/Peregrinajes: Theorizing Coalition Against Multiple Oppressions*. New York: Rowman & Littlefield.

Lugones, María (2006) 'On Complex Communication', *Hypatia*, 21 (3): 75–85.

Mahowald, Mary Briody (ed.) [1977] (1994) *Philosophy of Woman*. New York: Hackett.

Mahowald, Mary Briody (1996) *Women and Children in Health Care: An Unequal Majority*. Oxford: Oxford University Press.

Mahowald, Mary Briody (2000) *Genes, Women and Equity*. Oxford: Oxford University Press.

Mahowald, Mary Briody (2004) 'Prenatal Testing', *Hypatia*, 19 (3): 216–21.

Matsuda, Mari J. and Charles, Lawrence (1993) *Words That Wound: Critical Race Theory, Assaultive Speech, and the First Amendment*. Boulder, CO: Westview Press.

Mayberry, M. (2001) *Feminist Science Studies*. New York: Routledge.

McWhorter, Ladelle (1999) *Bodies and Pleasures*. Bloomington, IN: Indiana University Press.

Merchant, Caroline (1980) *The Death of Nature*. San Francisco: Harper Books.

Mill, John Stuart (2002) *The Basic Writings of John Stuart Mill: On Liberty, the Subjection of Women and Utilitarianism*. New York: Modern Library.

Millet, Kate [1970] (2000) *Sexual Politics*. Chicago: University of Illinois Press.

Mills, Charles (1999) *The Racial Contract*. Ithaca, NY: Cornell University Press.

Mitchell, Juliet (1972) *Women's Estate*. New York: Pantheon Books.

Mitchell, Juliet (1974) *Psychoanalysis and Feminism*. New York: Basic Books.

Mitchell, Juliet (1984) *Women, the Longest Revolution: Essays on Feminism, Literature, and Psychoanalysis*. New York: Virago.

Mitchell, Juliet (2001) *Madmen and Medusa: Reclaiming Hysteria*. New York: Basic Books.

Mitchell, Juliet (2003) *Siblings: Sex and Violence*. Cambridge: Polity Press.

Mohanty, Chanda Talpade (2003) *Feminism Without Borders: Decolonizing Theory, Practicing Solidarity*. Durham, NC: Duke University Press.

Mohanty, Chandra Talpade and Alexander, M. Jacqui (eds) (1996) *Feminist Genealogies, Colonial Legacies, Democratic Futures*. New York: Routledge.

Mohanty, Chadra Talpade et al. (eds) (1991) *Third World Women and the Politics of Feminism*. Bloomington, IN: Indiana University Press.

Moi, Toril (1994) *Simone de Beauvoir: The Making of an Intellectual Woman*. New York: Blackwell Publishers.

Moraga, Cherríe and Anzaldúa, Gloria (eds) (1981) *This Bridge Called My Back: Writings By Radical Women of Color*. Berkeley, CA: 3rd Woman Press.

Morris, Sherri Groveman (2006) 'DSD But Intersex Too: Shifting Paradigms Without Abandoning Roots', online at: www.isna.org.

Narayan, Uma (1997) *Dislocating Cultures: Identities, Traditions, and Third-World Feminism*. New York: Routledge.

Narayan, Uma and Bartkowiak, Julia J. (eds) (1999) *Having and Raising Children: Unconventional Families, Hard Choices, and the Social Good*. State College, PA: Pennsylvania State University Press.

Narayan, Uma and Harding, Sandra (eds) (2002) *Decentering the Center: Philosophy for a Multicultural, Postcolonial, and Feminist World*. Bloomington, IN: Indiana University Press.

Narayan, Uma and Shanley, Mary (1997) *Reconstructing Political Theory: Feminist Perspectives*. State College, PA: Pennsylvania State University Press.

Nelson, Jennifer (2003) *Women of Color and the Reproductive Rights Movement*. New York: New York University Press.

Nelson, Lynn Hankinson (1989) *Who Knows? From Quine to a Feminist Empiricism*. Philadelphia: Temple University Press.

Nicholson, Linda (ed.) (1997) *The Second Wave*. New York: Routledge.

Noddings, Nel (2003) *Caring: A Feminine Approach to Ethics and Moral Education*. Berkeley, CA: University of California Press.

Noddings, Nel (2004) *Happiness and Education*. Cambridge: Cambridge University Press.

Noddings, Nel (2006a) *Critical Lessons: What Our Schools Should Teach*. Cambridge: Cambridge University Press.

Noddings, Nel (2006b) *Starting at Home: Caring and Social Policy*. Cambridge: Cambridge University Press.

Nussbaum, Martha (1992) *Love's Knowledge: Essays on Philosophy and Literature*. Oxford: Oxford University Press.

Nussbaum, Martha (2000) *Sex and Social Justice*. Oxford: Oxford University Press.

Nussbaum, Martha (2001) *Women and Human Development: The Capabilities Approach*. Cambridge: Cambridge University Press.

Nussbaum, Martha (2004) *Hiding from Humanity: Disgust, Shame, and the Law*. Princeton, NJ: Princeton University Press.

Nye, Robert A. (ed.) (1999) *Sexuality*. Oxford: Oxford University Press.

Okin, Susan Moller (1979) *Women in Western Political Thought*. Princeton, NJ: Princeton University Press.

Okin, Susan Moller (1989) *Justice, Gender and the Family*. New York: Basic Books.

Okin, Susan Moller (1999) *Is Multi-Culturalism Bad for Women?* Princeton, NJ: Princeton University Press.

Omi, Michael and Winant, Howard (1994) *Racial Formation in the United States: From the 1960s to the 1990s*. New York: Routledge.

Pateman, Carole (1988) *The Sexual Contract*. Stanford, CA: Stanford University Press.

Pateman, Carole (1990) *The Disorder of Women*. Stanford, CA: Stanford University Press.

Penrod, Lynn (1996) *Hélène Cixous*. New York: Twayne.

Plumwood, Val (1994) *Feminism and the Mastery of Nature*. New York: Routledge.

Plumwood, Val (2002) *Environmental Culture: The Ecological Crisis of Reason*. New York: Routledge.

Potter, Elizabeth (2001) *Gender and Boyle's Law of Gases*. Bloomington, IN: Indiana University Press.

Potter, Elizabeth and Alcoff, Linda Martín (eds) (1991) *Feminist Epistemologies*. New York: Routledge.

Probyn, Elspeth (1993) *Sexing the Self*. New York: Routledge.

Probyn, Elspeth (1996) *Outside Belongings*. New York: Routledge.

Probyn, Elspeth (2000) *Carnal Appetites: FoodSexIdentities*. New York: Routledge.

Probyn, Elspeth (2005) *Blush: Faces of Shame*. Minneapolis, MN: University of Minnesota Press.

Purdy, Laura M. (1978) 'Genetic Diseases: Can Having Children be Immoral?', in John Buckley (ed.), *Genetics Now: Ethical Issues in Genetic Research*. New York: University Press of America, pp. 25–39.

Rowland, Robyn (1992) *Living Laboratories: Women and Reproductive Technologies*. Bloomington, IN: Indiana University Press.

Ruddick, Sara (1989) *Maternal Thinking: Toward a Politics of Peace*. New York: Ballantine.

Ruether, Rosemary Radford (1975) *New Woman, New Earth: Sexist Ideologies and Human Liberation*. New York: Seabury Press.

Sandoval, Chela (1990) 'Feminism and Racism: A Report on the 1981 National Women's Studies Association', in Gloria Anzaldúa (ed.), *Making Face, Making Soul/Haciendo Caras: Creative and Critical Perspectives by Feminists of Color*. San Francisco: Aunt Lute Books.

Sandoval, Chela (2000) *Methodology of the Oppressed*. Minneapolis, MN: University of Minnesota Press.

Schutte, Ofelia (1984) *Beyond Nihilism: Nietzsche without Masks*. Chicago: University of Chicago Press.

Schutte, Ofelia (1993) *Cultural Identity and Social Liberation in Latin American Thought*. Albany, NY: State University of New York Press.

Schutte, Ofelia (1998) 'Cultural Alterity: Cross-Cultural Communication and Feminist Thought in North-South Dialogue', *Hypatia*, 2: 53–72.

Seager, Joni (2003) *The Penguin Atlas of Women in the World*. New York: Penguin Books.

Seigfried, Charlene Haddock (1996) *Pragmatism and Feminism: Reweaving the Social Fabric*. Chicago: University of Chicago Press.

Shiva, Vandana (1993) *Monocultures of the Mind*. Boston: South End Press.

Shiva, Vandana (1997) *Biopiracy: The Plunder of Nature and Knowledge*. Boston: South End Press.

Shiva, Vandana (2000) *Stolen Harvest: The Hijacking of the Global Food Supply*. Boston: South End Press.

Shiva, Vandana (2002) *Water Wars: Privatization, Pollution, and Profit*. Boston: South End Press.

Shiva, Vandana (2005) *Earth Democracy: Justice, Sustainaibility, and Peace*. Boston: South End Press.

Shiva, Vandana and Mies, Maria (eds) (1993) *Ecofeminism*. New York: Zed Press.

Silvers, Anita (1989) *Puzzles About Art: An Aesthetics Casebook*. New York: St. Martin's Press.

Silvers, Anita and Rhodes, Rosamond (2002) *Medicine and Social Justice*. Oxford: Oxford University Press.

Silvers, Anita, Wasserman, David and Mahowald, Mary (1998) *Disabilty, Difference, Discrimination*. New York: Rowman & Littlefield.

Simons, Margaret (2000) *Beauvoir and 'The Second Sex'*. New York: Rowman & Littlefield.

Simons, Margaret (2006) *The Philosophy of Simone de Beauvoir*. Bloomington, IN: Indiana University Press.

Smith, Barbara (2000a) *Home Girls: A Black Feminist Anthology*. New Brunswick, NJ: Rutgers University Press.

Smith, Barbara (2000b) *The Truth That Never Hurts: Writings on Race, Gender, and Freedom*. New Brunswick, NJ: Rutgers University Press.

Spelman, Elizabeth (1990) *Inessential Woman: Problems of Exclusion in Feminist Thought*. Boston: Beacon Press.

Spelman, Elizabeth (2002) *Repair: The Impulse to Restore in a Fragile World*. Boston: Beacon Press.

Spivak, Gayatri Chakravorty (1988) 'Can the Subaltern Speak?', in Lawrence Grossberg (ed.), *Marxism and the Interpretation of Culture*. Chicago: University of Illinois Press, pp. 271–316.

Spivak, Gayatri Chakravorty (1993) *Outside In the Teaching Machine*. London: Routledge.

Spivak, Gayatri Chakravorty (1995) *The Spivak Reader: Selected Works of Gayatri Chakravorty Spivak*. New York: Routledge.

Spivak, Gayatri Chakravorty (1999) *A Critique of Post-Colonial Reason: Toward a History of the Vanishing Present*. Cambridge, MA: Harvard University Press.

Spivak, Gayatri Chakravorty (2003) *Death of a Discipline*. New York: Columbia University Press.

Spretnak, Charlene (ed.) (1982) *The Politics of Women's Spirituality: Essays on the Rise of Spiritual Power within the Feminist Movement*. New York: Anchor Books.

Sullivan, Shannon (2001) *Living Across and Through Skins: Transactional Bodies, Pragmatism, and Feminism*. Bloomington, IN: Indiana University Press.

Taylor Mill, Harriet Hardy (1998) *The Complete Works of Harriet Taylor Mill*. Bloomington, IN: Indiana University Press.

Thomas, Carol (2002) 'Disability Theory: Key Ideas, Issues and Thinkers', in Colin Barnes et al. (eds), *Disability Studies Today*. Oxford: Polity Press, pp. 38–57.

Thomson, Judith Jarvis (1971) 'A Defense of Abortion', *Philosophy and Public Affairs*, 1 (1): 47.

Tong, Rosemarie Putnam (1997) *Feminist Approaches to Bioethics*. Boulder, CO: Westview Press.

Tong, Rosemarie Putnam (1998) *Feminist Thought: A More Comprehensive Introduction*. Boulder, CO: Westview Press.

Tong, Rosemarie Putnam and Tuana, Nancy (1994) *Feminist Philosophy: Essential Readings in Theory, Reinterpretation, and Application*. Boulder, CO: Westview Press.

Tremain, Shelley (2005) *Foucault and the Government of Disability*. Ann Arbor, MI: University of Michigan Press.

Tuana, Nancy (ed.) (1989) *Feminism and Science*. Bloomington, IN: Indiana University Press.

Tuana, Nancy (1992) *Women and the History of Philosophy*. New York: Paragon House.

Tuana, Nancy (1993) *The Less Noble Sex*. Bloomington, IN: Indiana University Press.

Tuana, Nancy (2001a) *Revealing Male Bodies*. Bloomington, IN: Indiana University Press.

Tuana, Nancy (2001b) *enGendering Rationalities*. New York: SUNY Press.

Waithe, Mary Ellen (2003) *History of Women Philosophers, volumes I–IV*. New York: Springer.

Walker, Alice (1983) *In Search of Our Mother's Gardens: Womanist Prose*. New York: Harvest Press.

Warren, Karen (2000) *Ecofeminist Philosophy*. New York: Rowman & Littlefield.

Warren, Mary Anne (2000) *Moral Status: Obligations to Persons and Other Living Things*. New York: Oxford University Press.

Weiss, Gail (1999) *Perspectives on Embodiment*. New York: Routledge.

Wendell, Susan (1996) *The Rejected Body*. New York: Routledge.

Williams, Christine (2002) 'Sexual Harassment and Sadomasochism', *Hypatia*, 17 (2): 99–117.

Wollstonecraft, Mary [1792] (1988) *A Vindication of the Rights of Woman*. New York: W. W. Norton.

Young, Iris Marion (1980) 'Throwing Like a Girl: A Phenomenology of Feminine Body Comportment, Motility, and Spatiality', *Human Studies*, 3: 137–56.

Young, Iris Marion (1990) *Justice and the Politics of Difference*. Princeton, NJ: Princeton University Press.

Young, Iris Marion (1997) *Intersecting Voices*. Princeton, NJ: Princeton University Press.

Young, Iris Marion (2002) *Inclusion and Democracy*. Oxford: Oxford University Press.

Young, Iris Marion (2005) *On Female Body Experience: 'Throwing Like a Girl' and Other Essays*. New York: Oxford University Press.

Zack, Naomi (1994) *Race and Mixed Race*. Philadelphia: Temple University Press.

Zack, Naomi (1996) *Bachelors of Science: Seventeenth-Century Identity, Then and Now*. Philadelphia: Temple University Press.

Zack, Naomi (2002) *Philosophy of Race and Science*. New York: Routledge.

Zack, Naomi (2005) *Inclusive Feminism: A Third Wave Theory of Women's Commonality*. New York: Rowman & Littlefield.

Zippel, Kathrin S. (2006) *The Politics of Sexual Harassment: A Comparative Study of the United States, the European Union, and Germany*. Cambridge: Cambridge University Press.